THE
RED
BARON

THE
RED
BARON

A PHOTOGRAPHIC ALBUM OF THE FIRST
WORLD WAR'S GREATEST ACE,
MANFRED VON RICHTHOFEN

TERRY C. TREADWELL

AIR WORLD

THE RED BARON
A Photographic Album of the First World War's Greatest Ace, Manfred von Richthofen

First published in Great Britain in 2021 by
Air World
An imprint of
Pen & Sword Books Ltd
Yorkshire – Philadelphia

Copyright © Terry C. Treadwell, 2021

ISBN 978 1 52678 132 1

The right of Terry C. Treadwell to be identified as Author of this work has been asserted by him in accordance with the Copyright, Designs and Patents Act 1988.

A CIP catalogue record for this book is available from the British Library.

All rights reserved. No part of this book may be reproduced or transmitted in any form or by any means, electronic or mechanical including photocopying, recording or by any information storage and retrieval system, without permission from the Publisher in writing.

Typeset by SJmagic DESIGN SERVICES, India.
Printed and bound in the UK by CPI.

Pen & Sword Books Limited incorporates the imprints of Atlas, Archaeology, Aviation, Discovery, Family History, Fiction, History, Maritime, Military, Military Classics, Politics, Select, Transport, True Crime, Air World, Frontline Publishing, Leo Cooper, Remember When, Seaforth Publishing, The Praetorian Press, Wharncliffe Local History, Wharncliffe Transport, Wharncliffe True Crime and White Owl.

For a complete list of Pen & Sword titles please contact

PEN & SWORD BOOKS LIMITED
47 Church Street, Barnsley, South Yorkshire, S70 2AS, England
E-mail: enquiries@pen-and-sword.co.uk
Website: www.pen-and-sword.co.uk

Or
PEN AND SWORD BOOKS
1950 Lawrence Rd, Havertown, PA 19083, USA
E-mail: Uspen-and-sword@casematepublishers.com
Website: www.penandswordbooks.com

Contents

Introduction vii

Chapter One 1
Chapter Two 46

Post Mortem of Richthofen.. 128
Appendix I: List of Manfred von Richthofen's victories in the
              First World War 141
Appendix II: Rittmeister Manfred Freiherr von Richthofen 147

Glossary 149
Index 150

Introduction

Of the millions of Germans who died in the First World War, just under 7,000 were members of the German Army Air Service. Comparatively very little has been written about this section of the German military, and of this, more has been written about one person than any other, Rittmeister Manfred Freiherr von Richthofen: The Red Baron. He has been debated, argued about and demonised, but one thing that is certain is that he was without doubt one of the most talked about charismatic figures of his time. His deadly skill as a fighter pilot was endorsed by the eighty victories or 'kills' he achieved in a very short time span of just twenty months, and when only 25 years old.

Manfred von Richthofen was born into an aristocratic Prussian family and enjoyed a very privileged lifestyle. This book does not try and tell the story of his life in depth, but gives an insight, by way of photographs, into how this remarkable young man achieved a highly respected place in military history.

Chapter One

When the Bosnian-Serb activist Gavrilo Princip pulled the trigger on his revolver and assassinated Archduke Ferdinand, the heir to the Austro-Hungarian throne, it lit the fuse that was to ignite the time bomb that had been waiting to explode in Europe for a number of years. It plunged Europe, and other countries, into a costly, savage war, both in human lives and economically.

The Austro-Hungarians were in control of Sarajevo, the capital of Bosnia, and subsequently controlled the rest of the country. Bosnia was supported by the Serbians, the majority of whom lived in and around

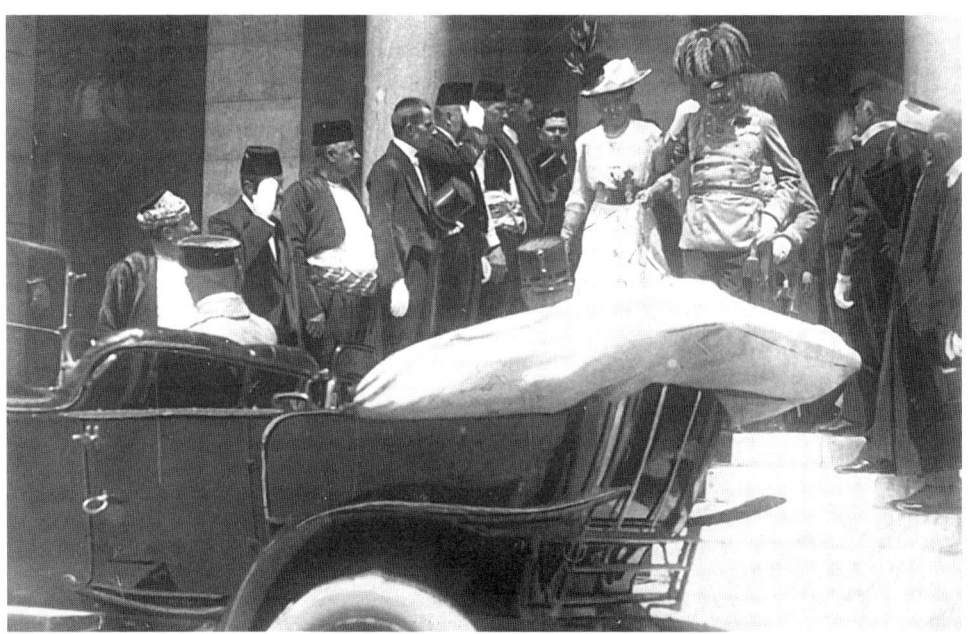

Archduke Ferdinand and his wife about to enter their car minutes before being assassinated by Gavrilo Princip.

THE RED BARON

Gavrilo Princip being arrested moments after he had shot and killed the Archduke Ferdinand.

Bosnia. There had always been unrest in Bosnia with regard to the Austro-Hungarians governing the country, and when the assassination took place, the Austro-Hungarians threatened to take revenge on the Bosnian/Serbian people. However, the Russians declared that they would support Serbia in any action taken by the Austro-Hungarians. This meant that if the Austrians attacked Serbia, the Russians would take the Serbian side, thus opening hostilities between the two major powers.

Germany supported the Austro-Hungarian Empire through a defence treaty and stated that it would support Austria in the event of an attack by Serbia or Russia. At this point, the French joined in saying that they had a treaty with Russia and would back them in the event of any hostilities taking place. Britain had no such treaty, although they backed the French verbally and refused to get involved until the Germans announced that they would attack France by going through Belgium. Britain, which had a treaty with Belgium, stepped in saying that it would support the Belgian people if their country were to be invaded. One of the main reasons Britain supported Belgium was that it did not want either Germany or France dominating the entire coastline that faced Britain. Within months, almost the whole of

CHAPTER ONE

Europe was at war and it was against this background that the legend of the Red Baron was born – Rittmeister Manfred Freiherr von Richthofen.

On 2 May 1892, Baroness Kunigunde von Richthofen gave birth to a boy who was to become a household name in Germany and throughout the world for years to come – Manfred von Richthofen. There was nothing special about Manfred: he was an ordinary boy, small in stature with blond hair. He enjoyed a privileged lifestyle, being privately tutored at home until he was 9, before being sent to a school in Schweidnitz. At the age of 11, he was enrolled as a cadet in the military school at Wahlstatt. He was not consulted about this and was not particularly eager to join the military, but it was his father's wish that he follow in the family tradition. His father had been a major in the Leib-Kürassier Regiment but had had to retire because of deafness contracted after he had dived, fully clothed, into an icy river to help rescue three soldiers from his regiment.

7 year old Manfred von Richthofen

Richthofen Coat of Arms

Above left: A young Manfred von Richthofen as a cadet.

Above right: Cadet Manfred von Richthofen with his brother Lothar and sister Ilse.

The sudden transition from a privileged lifestyle to the austere, grim, disciplined confines of a military school was a huge shock to Manfred. His academic achievements there were unremarkable, but he excelled in all the physical activities available to him. After six years at the school he was sent to the Royal Military Academy at Lichterfelde for a year, followed by a further year at the Berlin War Academy before being commissioned in 1912 as a Leutnant in the 1st Regiment of Uhlans Kaiser Alexander III, which was essentially a cavalry outfit.

Life in the regiment was fine until August 1914 when war broke out and his regiment was sent to the Front.

The following year was spent living in dugouts and crawling through mud-filled trenches to deliver messages. The realisation that there was no need for cavalry soon became apparent, as the battlefields were pitted with large shell holes, covered in barbed wire entanglements and any cavalry charge would be mown down with machine-gun fire, so all the training with lance and sword was useless. In a letter home Manfred wrote:

> *'I am now the Assistant Adjutant of the 18th Infantry Brigade and at last seeing some action.'*

But sporadic action was not enough for Manfred, and, after seeing aircraft buzzing overhead on a number of occasions, he applied for a transfer to

CHAPTER ONE

Right: Manfred von Richthofen with fellow members of the 3rd Eskadron Uhlans. Manfred is third one down in centre.

Below: Uhlan Regiment moving towards the Front Line at the beginning of the war.

the newly formed Fliegertruppe (Air Service). His first application was refused, but after repeated efforts it was accepted and he was posted to FEA (Feldflieger Abteilung) 7, Köln (Cologne) for training as an observer.

Germany's Air Service at the time was in a massive state of flux, brought about by the fact that Germany thought that the war would be a very short one. They were not ready for a long, ever-changing war of attrition and were frantically trying to build an air force. Training for an observer was normally about twelve to eighteen months, but such was the demand for observers that Manfred von Richthofen spent just two weeks initial training before being posted to FEA 6 for further training by

Left: A young Manfred von Richthofen with fellow observers during training.

Below: Manfred (L) with fellow observers Leutnants Freiherr von Könitz, Freiherr Hans Haller von Hallerstein and unknown during training.

Freepost Plus RTKE-RGRJ-KTTX
Pen & Sword Books Ltd
47 Church Street
BARNSLEY
S70 2AS

DISCOVER MORE ABOUT PEN & SWORD BOOKS

Pen & Sword Books have over 4000 books currently available, our imprints include: Aviation, Naval, Military, Archaeology, Transport, Frontline, Seaforth and the Battleground series, and we cover all periods of history on land, sea and air.

Can we stay in touch? From time to time we'd like to send you our latest catalogues, promotions and special offers by post. If you would prefer not to receive these, please tick this box. ☐

We also think you'd enjoy some of the latest products and offers by post from our trusted partners: companies operating in the clothing, collectables, food & wine, gardening, gadgets & entertainment, health & beauty, household goods, and home interiors categories. If you would like to receive these by post, please tick this box. ☐

We respect your privacy. We use personal information you provide us with to send you information about our products, maintain records and for marketing purposes. For more information explaining how we use your information please see our privacy policy at www.pen-and-sword.co.uk/privacy. You can opt out of our mailing list at any time via our website or by calling 01226 734222.

Mr/Mrs/Ms ....

Postcode.......................... Email address...

Address...

Website: www.pen-and-sword.co.uk Email: enquiries@pen-and-sword.co.uk
Telephone: 01226 734555 Fax: 01226 734438
Stay in touch: facebook.com/penandswordbooks or follow us on Twitter @penswordbooks

CHAPTER ONE

experience. His map reading and reconnaissance training, whilst with the Uhlan regiment, no doubt stood him in good stead. He was then posted first to A.Fl.Pk from where he was posted to his new unit, Feldflieger Abteilung (FEA) 69, commanded by Hauptmann Kurt Müller. Here he was assigned as an observer with Oberleutnant Georg Zeumer as his pilot.

Jagdstaffel of Kaghol 1. L–R: Leutnant Schramm, Oberleutnant Bethge, Leutnant Georg Zeumer, Unknown, Leutnant Parschau.

This aircraft AEG G.II flown by Leutnant Georg Zeumer was one of the first aircraft in which Manfred von Richthofen flew as an observer.

A picture of a youthful-looking Manfred von Richthofen taken in the early years as a fighter pilot.

Such was the demand for observers that he flew with several different pilots, which didn't bother Manfred as long as he was flying. On one mission, he was assigned to fly with Oberleutnant Holck, and as they flew through a thick cloud of black smoke billowing out from the burning village of Wiczniace it caused the engine to lose power, forcing them to fly lower. As they emerged from the smoke, they came under heavy and intense ground fire from retreating Russian soldiers. Holck managed to get back over their lines before putting the badly damaged aircraft on the ground. This was Richthofen's first real encounter with the enemy as an airman, but it would not be the last. Manfred von Richthofen's stay at FA 59 was short-lived and he soon received a posting to BAO (Brieftauben-Abteilung-Ostende).

On arriving at the airfield at Ghistelles, south of Ostend, he was delighted to meet up with Oberleutnant Georg Zeumer who had also been posted there some weeks earlier. The two men became friends and flew a number of missions together, hunting enemy aircraft and carrying out bombing raids. But their relationship wasn't always that amicable as there were a number of occasions when one of them would verbally berate the other on incidents that happened when on a mission. On one mission, Manfred von Richthofen spotted what he thought was a submarine just below the surface. After pointing it out to Zeumer, they followed it for a short while, but Zeumer decided that if it was a submarine they had no way of knowing whether it was a German or a British one, so left the area – much to the annoyance of Richthofen who wanted to pursue it. On another occasion they encountered a Farman MF.II on a reconnaissance flight and attacked it. Their aircraft received numerous hits whilst the Farman appeared to get away unscathed. Zeumer blamed Richthofen's marksmanship, whilst Richthofen blamed

CHAPTER ONE

Zeumer's ability to fly under combat conditions. Despite all this the two men remained amicable and continued to fly as a team.

During quiet periods, Zeumer started to teach Manfred von Richthofen how to fly, but the arrival of one of the new single-seat Fokker Eindeckers gave Zeumer more opportunities to fly solo missions. This of course meant that Richthofen spent less time flight training, something he desperately wanted to do, and so it was inevitable that he would be teamed up with someone else as an observer, but only occasionally able to continue his flight training with Zeumer.

In April 1915, General von Einen, Commander of the 3rd Army, became increasingly concerned with the build-up of the French army close to his thinly held front line. He had at his disposal just four Feldflieger-Abteilungs, (Nos. 10, 20, 22 and 53) with a total of just twenty-seven aircraft. By the end of September the number of aircraft had increased to over forty, just in time for the start of the Champagne action. Manfred von Richthofen was assigned to fly with Oberleutnant von Osterroht as his observer, and it was whilst on one mission that he got his first taste of victory. Flying over the front line, their aircraft encountered a Farman S.II and attacked. After firing a short burst at the Farman, Richthofen's guns jammed, but after frantically working to clear the blockage, he managed to send a long burst into the enemy aircraft, then watched it plunge towards the ground and crash behind its own lines. Unfortunately Manfred von Richthofen failed to record the date and the place and for some unknown reason no claim was made, as it would have almost certainly been accepted.

At the beginning of October 1915, Manfred von Richthofen met Hauptmann Oswald Boelcke, Germany's top fighter pilot, a meeting that was to have far reaching effects.

The meeting with Boelcke spurred Richthofen into continuing his flying lessons with Zeumer. Within weeks of meeting Boelcke,

Portrait shot of Leutnant Oswald Boelcke.

THE RED BARON

Manfred von Richthofen took his first solo flight and, unsurprisingly, crashed on landing.

Unhurt and undaunted he continued and two weeks later applied for his official flight test. Despite carrying out the test without a problem, or so he thought, the examiner, Hauptmann Freiherr von Thüna, decided he wasn't ready and failed him.

Disappointed, but still full of resolve, Manfred von Richthofen continued to fly as an observer with Oberleutnant von Osterroht throughout the Champagne battle.

He continued with his unofficial flight training with Georg Zeumer when possible, but in November the two of them received orders to go to Ghistelles and then to Berlin. Manfred von Richthofen immediately requested a transfer to the flight school at Döberitz to continue his flying training, this time officially. This was granted and on Christmas Day 1915,

Hauptmann Paul Henning von Osterroht, commander of Jasta 12 with Manfred von Richthofen looking at Manfred's Albatros D.III. The pilot behind is Unteroffizier Gille. This was the time in April 1917 that Jasta 11 joined with Jasta 12 at Epinoy airfield for a joint mission.

CHAPTER ONE

Manfred von Richthofen and Hauptmann Paul Henning von Osterroht poring over a map to discuss the next possible mission.

This photograph was taken on 15 April 1917 at Epinoy airfield when Jasta 11 and Jasta 12 joined together for a mission. L–R: Leutnant Schock, Leutnant Bevar, Hauptmann Paul von Osterroht, Vizefeldwebel Grigo and Manfred von Richthofen. Richthofen is seen wearing his well-worn leather flying jacket and his fur-lined flying helmet.

after weeks of rigorous training and tests, he passed his final flying exam and was awarded his pilot's badge, becoming a Flugzeugführer.

In March 1916, Manfred von Richthofen was posted to Kaghol (KG) 2 Kasta 8 located at Mont-Murville about 35 miles from Verdun.

The commanding officer of Kasta 8, Hauptmann Victor Carganico, welcomed him and then told him that he would have to set about finding his own mechanic.

Left: Richthofen's German army pilot badge.

Below: Mont Murville where the Kaghol's 2 Kastas were based.

CHAPTER ONE

Fortune smiled upon him when he met an infantryman/motor mechanic by the name of Josef Holzapfel, who was to remain as his trusted mechanic, alongside his orderly, Corporal Menzke, until that fateful day in April 1918. It was around this time that he acquired his Great Dane, Moritz, who also remained a faithful companion.

Above left: Manfred von Richthofen deep in conversation with Staffelführer Victor Carganico.

Above right: Excellent shot of Richthofen in the cockpit of his Albatros D.V about to taxi out with his mechanic Josef Holzapfel holding down the tail. (Cover picture)

Manfred von Richthofen with his dog Moritz at Lechelle with Leutnant Erich Lowenhardt

THE RED BARON

Manfred von Richthofen with his dog Moritz.

Above left: A delightful informal photograph of Manfred von Richthofen with his Great Dane Moritz.

Above right: Informal shot of Manfred von Richthofen with his Great Dane Moritz.

CHAPTER ONE

Above: Kampfgeschwadern 2 members with a young Manfred von Richthofen fourth from the right in the front row.

Right: Manfred von Richthofen with his Great Dane Mortz.

Below: Manfred von Richthofen with L–R: Unknown, Hauptmann Carganico and Leutnant Alfred Gerstenberg.

THE RED BARON

Flying a slow, cumbersome LVG C.II, Richthofen was thrown into the forefront of the battle of Verdun. This was a far bloodier battle than the Champagne action, and the Fliegertruppe lost more than eight aircraft in the first six weeks of the battle. On 25 April 1916, Richthofen claimed his first victory when he shot down a Nieuport II west of Douaumont, but again this was not confirmed. KG2's main role was to carry out escort duties and aerial blockade missions, which meant that only on the odd occasion did they get involved in a dogfight. The LVG C.II was replaced by Roland C.II 'Walfisch', which was not a great deal different from the LVG. But when Fokker and Pfalz E Types suddenly became available, both the KGs had fighter capabilities.

It was decided to take almost all the Fokker Eindeckers from KG1 and KG2 and create two fighter units called KEKs (Kampfeinsitzerkommandos). Two single-seat Fokker Eindeckers remained with KG1 and KG2, which enabled Manfred von Richthofen and Leutnant Hans Reimann to go on 'hunting' expeditions, when not on other duties. But Hans Reimann was

Above left: A relaxed-looking Manfred von Richthofen seen here returning from a mission.

Above right: A young Manfred von Richthofen wrapped up against the cold.

CHAPTER ONE

shot down close to the French lines and barely escaped with his life; the replacement aircraft, flown by Richthofen a few days later, was wrecked when the engine failed on take-off.

Manfred von Richthofen and Hans Reimann found themselves back flying the two-seater Roland C.II for the next few months.

In June 1916, the German High Command ended its attacks on Verdun in an effort to shore up the Eastern Front where the Russians

Above: Richthofen's Fokker E.III being righted after crashing on take-off.

Below: Manfred von Richthofen's Fokker E.III nose down after his Oberursal engine failed on take-off.

were massing and also the Somme where the British and French were preparing for an assault. KG2 quietly decamped and left the area aboard several trains and headed for Kowel (Kovel) on the Eastern Front. The pilots had left their previous aircraft behind and were now flying Albatros C.IIs and Rumpler C.Is, all fitted with machine guns and infinitely more reliable.

KG2 found itself restricted to flying bombing or reconnaissance missions, which pleased Richthofen because it increased his flying time.

For the next few months, Richthofen flew as many missions as he could, then word came through that Hauptmann Oswald Boelcke was to visit and that he was to lead one of the new fighter units. The main reason for Boelcke's visit was to see his older brother Wilhelm, who was CO of Kasta 10, but a rumour circulated that he was also looking for pilots for his new Staffel. Then out of the blue Oswald Boelcke asked for Leutnant Böhme and Leutnant Manfred von Richthofen to be assigned to his Staffel. Both Böhme and Richthofen were delighted and immediately accepted the chance to fly with Germany's top fighter pilot. Oswald Boelcke, in the meantime, had been give orders to establish his new Jagdstaffel 2 at Bertincourt, a small village some 20 miles outside of Cambrai. However, this caused a problem: because of the relentless pressure by the British it was discovered that they were less than 5 miles

A young Manfred von Richthofen standing in front of his Albatros D.III at Roucourt in April 1917.

CHAPTER ONE

from the front line. Oswald Boelcke arrived at Bertincourt at the end of August to discover that FFl.Abt. 32 had gone to Sains-les-Marquion, but fortunately had left behind wooden aircraft hangars surrounded by trees, which gave them perfect camouflage from the air. In front of the hangars was a neatly mowed, flat meadow providing the Staffel with an excellent landing and take-off area.

Richthofen and Böhme arrived at Jasta 2 on 1 September 1916 to find that there were only three aircraft for seven pilots, including Oswald Boelcke. Slowly the number of pilots and aircraft increased until every pilot was able to share an aircraft.

In the middle of September 1916, Oswald Boelcke led Manfred von Richthofen and Erwin Böhme on a 'hunting' trip and encountered a flight of Sopwith 1½ Strutters from 70 Squadron, RFC. Boelcke claimed one and although both Richthofen and Böhme scored hits on two others, they were unsuccessful in achieving a 'kill', but they were learning combat techniques from the master. The following day, the same trio fought again and this

Above left: Manfred von Richthofen being dressed for a mission.

Above right: Manfred von Richthofen using a ladder to get into the cockpit of his Albatros D.III. Note the unpainted patched bullet hole in the fuselage aft of the cockpit.

Jasta 2 pilots in November 1916. L–R: Leutnant Sandel, Offizierstellvertreter. Max Muller, Leutnant Manfred von Richthofen, Leutnant Guenther, Oberleutnant Kirmaier, Leutnant Hans Immelmann, Leutnant Koenig, Leutnant Hoehne, Leutnant Wortman and Leutnant Collin.

Leutnant Oswald Boelcke talking to Leutnant Hoehne from the cockpit of a DH.2 of 24 Squadron RFC, that he had earlier shot down while Manfred von Richthofen looks on.

CHAPTER ONE

Leutnant Oswald Boelcke with friends including an unusually shy Manfred von Richthofen standing at the back of the group marked with an X.

Crowd of pilots greet Hauptmann Boelcke as he gets down from his Albatros D.II at Lagnicourt. L–R: Leutnant Erwin Böhme, Oberleutnant Stefan Kirmaier, Leutnant Manfred von Richthofen, Wortmann, Oberleutnant Gunther, König, Müller and Höhne.

time Boelcke got two, one a DH2 of 24 Squadron RFC, but Richthofen and Böhme were again unsuccessful.

Hauptmann Oswald Boelcke was becoming increasingly frustrated with the lack of aircraft and, in an attempt to try and hurry things along, sent some of his pilots to the Albatros factory, but to no avail. Despite his angry exchanges with High Command regarding his request for new aircraft, nothing seemed to happen, but then a phone call changed everything: his persistence had paid off, he was to receive six new Albatros D.Is and D.IIs for his Staffel. He immediately sent six pilots to collect them and fly them to Bertincourt.

Manfred von Richthofen preparing for a flight in an Albatros C.IX. Very few of this model aircraft were built.

This FE2b of No.11 Squadron, RFC flown by Lieutenant Morris and Lieutenant Rees was Manfred von Richthofen's first victory. The British crew managed to land the aircraft before dying of their wounds.

CHAPTER ONE

On 17 September, Jasta 2 were airborne again and this time Manfred von Richthofen scored his first confirmed victory, a FE.2b of 11 Squadron, RFC. As he watched the stricken aircraft plunge towards the ground, another German fighter appeared and started to attack; fortunately both Boelcke and a Leutnant Pelzer had witnessed his 'kill' so it was confirmed.

Manfred von Richthofen continued to add to his tally but there were some serious losses from Jasta 2. Leutnant Hans Reimann had just scored his fourth victory when he was rammed by a Martinsyde G.102 and fell to his death, and Leutnant Winand Grafe was shot down by a BE.12.

At the end of the September Richthofen's tally stood at three and Jasta 2 had been moved to Lagincourt.

In October 1916, Richthofen was flying a patrol near Bapaume when he attacked a BE.12 that was returning from an attack on the German lines. When he returned and made his claim, he was told that another pilot, Vizefeldwebel Mueller of Jasta 5, had already claimed the 'kill'. Richthofen was furious that anyone should even question his right to claim the victory. It was this arrogant, dogmatic attitude that would later not endear him to other pilots and sometimes bring into question his combat statements and claims.

Body of a German pilot lies grotesquely amongst the wreckage of his crashed Rumpler C.I. showing the horrors of war.

Said to be a photograph of a German pilot falling from his crippled, blazing Albatros D.III fighter. This could of course be a staged photograph, but even it is, it graphically shows the dangers that could befall pilots of all sides during the First World War and did on a number of occasions.

CHAPTER ONE

On 28 October, tragedy struck Jasta 2 when Hauptmann Oswald Boelcke was killed whilst pursuing a British aircraft together with his wingman Leutnant Erwin Böhme, just two days after scoring his fortieth victory.

In an attempt to avoid colliding with another British aircraft, which was being pursued by Manfred von Richthofen, he turned and collided with the undercarriage of Böhme's aircraft, ripping his upper wing apart. His Albatros D.II plunged to the ground, killing him instantly. This was a bitter blow to the German Air Service, and a tragic loss as he was considered to be Germany's first aerial tactician.

His funeral service was held in the cathedral at Cambrai and as the black-draped coffin left the cathedral, Leutnant Manfred von Richthofen led the mourners carrying Boelcke's Ordenkissen (medal pillow). The following day a lone British aircraft dropped a note that simply said:

> '*To the memory of Captain Boelcke, our brave and chivalrous opponent.' From the English Royal Flying Corps.*

Leutnant Stephan Kirmaier took Boelcke's place as CO of Jagdstaffel 2.

One month later he was killed when he was shot down. He was replaced by Hauptmann Walz, who remained as CO until August 1917 when he was replaced by Leutnant Erwin Böhme. In the meantime, Manfred von Richthofen continued to become the scourge of the allies as his victories

The body of Oswald Boelcke lying beside the wreckage of his aircraft.

Left: The body of Hauptmann Oswald Boelcke lying in state in the Gnarde Kirsche, Berlin.

Below: Manfred von Richthofen carrying the Ordenkissen at the funeral of his friend Oswald Boelcke.

CHAPTER ONE

Oberleutnant Stephan Kirmaier, Leutnant Hans Immelmann, Manfred von Richthofen and Leutnant Hans Wortman of Jasta 2 posing in front of Manfred's Albatros D.III.

continued to mount almost daily. He was rapidly coming to the notice of the German General Staff, who, after losing Oswald Boelcke, needed someone for the people to admire and Richthofen fitted the profile. As compensation for him not being given the Orden Pour le Mérite, he was awarded The Order of the House of Hohenzollern.

At the beginning of January 1917, Leutnant Manfred von Richthofen received orders from the General Staff telling him that he was now the CO of Jagdstaffel 11 at Douai. Richthofen was both annoyed and pleased: annoyed having to leave his beloved Jasta Boelcke, as it had become known, but pleased that he was now considered to be a leader. This was to be a challenge as Jagdstaffel 11 had been formed in September 1916 and had not scored one victory, whilst Richthofen now had sixteen 'kills' to his credit.

Richthofen openly admitted that he would rather have had the coveted Orden Pour le Mérite, something he thought he should have received earlier. Happily, shortly after arriving at Jagdstaffel 11, he received a telegram saying that the Kaiser had graciously awarded him the 'Blue Max' – the Orden Pour le Mérite.

THE RED BARON

Now aware of his responsibilities, he had to temper his driving ambition to become Germany's top fighter pilot (which in effect he already was), in order to develop his new command, a daunting task for a 24-year-old. To do this he felt he had to lead by example, and on 23 January he scored his seventeenth victory and Jagdstaffel 11's first. Vizefeldwebel Howe was accompanying him on this mission when they attacked a FE.8 of No.40 Squadron, RFC. After what seemed an interminable aerial battle, the aircraft was forced down. On landing, the pilot, Captain Greig and his observer Lieutenant MacLenna, were taken prisoner, but not before they managed to set fire to what was left of their aircraft. Richthofen also had to land because of a cracked wing, which he thought had been caused by machine-gun fire from another aircraft. The British crew were interrogated and told the German intelligence officer that they recognised the aircraft that had shot them down, calling it '*le petit rouge*', an aircraft that was becoming very well known to the allies. This was because Richthofen had had parts of his aircraft painted red so that his own men could easily identify him during a dogfight.

One week later, with Leutnant Allmenröder as his wingman, Richthofen, flying a Halberstadt D.II instead of his Fokker D.II, came across a BE.2e of No.16 RFC, artillery spotting. Despite having only one machine gun, which was mounted to the port side fuselage, he managed to close within 50 metres without being observed, and shot it down. The aircraft crash-landed behind

Front three-quarter view of the Fokker Dr.I Triplane flown by Manfred von Richthofen when only parts of the aircraft were painted red.

CHAPTER ONE

An excellent rare shot of Manfred von Richthofen landing his Fokker Dr.I Triplane.

German lines and both members of the crew were taken prisoner.

The weather turned sour at the beginning of February, restricting Jagdstaffel 11's missions, but on 14 February, the weather cleared and Richthofen, flying back from a meeting at Jagdstaffel Boelcke, encountered a BE.2d from No.2 Squadron, RFC, artillery spotting. Diving into attack he again closed within 50 metres before being spotted, but by then it was too late and Richthofen sent a long burst of machine-gun fire into the aircraft.

Trailing smoke, the aircraft plunged to the ground, killing the pilot, Lieutenant C. Bennett and badly injuring the observer 2nd Lieutenant Croft, who was taken prisoner. This, Richthofen's twentieth victory, increased his popularity with the German people.

A young Manfred von Richthofen standing in front of the wreckage of one of his victims.

THE RED BARON

The Jasta had now been equipped with the new Albatros D.III and Manfred von Richthofen had parts of his aircraft painted red, which meant that every time he went into combat he could be identified, not only by his own men but by the enemy. He started to train his men in the art of combat flying and soon had a Jasta that was up to the task. On the same day as he gained his twentieth victory, he shot down a BE.2d of No. 2 Squadron, RFC. Richthofen followed the aircraft down and watched it crash into the trenches over the British lines. Although there was no one to verify the 'kill', his word was accepted, such was the propaganda machine's desire to help and increase the fame of Manfred von Richthofen.

As his score mounted, the German propaganda machine got to work and soon the name of Rittmeister Freiherr Manfred von Richthofen became a household name and the idol of the young people of Germany. He became inundated with letters, mostly from young ladies, asking for photographs of him.

Above left: A young-looking Manfred von Richthofen wearing his Pour le Merite.

Above right: Black and white Sanke photograph of Manfred von Richthofen wearing some of his medals.

CHAPTER ONE

Above left: Studio portrait photograph of Manfred von Richthofen.

Above right: A portrait shot of Manfred von Richthofen of the type given to the public.

Right: A casual-looking Manfred von Richthofen with a cigarette in his hand.

Above left: Head and shoulders portrait shot of Manfred von Richthofen.

Above right: Manfred and Lothar von Richthofen caught in a relaxed moment.

Left: Portrait shot of Manfred von Richthofen wearing his fur flying suit.

CHAPTER ONE

Early shot of Manfred von Richthofen in a relaxing mood riding his bicycle.

Manfred von Richthofen an early 'Hell's Angel'.

THE RED BARON

Manfred von Richthofen aboard a train at Schweidnitz with a crowd of female admirers looking at him.

Manfred von Richthofen surrounded by a large group of young admirers.

CHAPTER ONE

Above left: Manfred von Richthofen talking with a young admirer. This picture gives a good indication of Richthofen's short stature.

Above right: Miniature portrait of Rittmeister Manfred Freiherr von Richthofen.

March 1917 was a disastrous month in the air for the Allies with a loss of 120 aircraft, but an extremely successful one for Manfred von Richthofen. In that one-month period, Richthofen shot down ten aircraft bringing his total of victories to thirty.

However, on 15 March, whilst on patrol, he suddenly came under attack from a British aircraft whose bullets punctured his engine and the wafer-thin fuel tanks on his aircraft. The moment he smelt the fuel spurting from the ruptured fuel tanks, he knew he had to get the aircraft on to the ground before it caught fire; he had seen many aircraft go down in flames, the crews dying horribly.

He immediately shut down the engine and looked for a place to put the damaged aircraft down. He found a small field near Henin Lietard, in Alsace and safely glided in.

The Battle for Arras at the beginning of April started with a massive air offensive by the British, who outnumbered the Germans by three to one.

One of Manfred von Richthofen's victims. The body of a French pilot lying in the wreckage of his aircraft.

Albatros D.III belonging to Jasta 11 being wheeled out of its hangar at Roucourt in April 1917.

CHAPTER ONE

Albatros D.III of Jasta 11 at Roucourt showing the damage to its propeller after its gun synchronization gear malfunctioned.

Jasta 11 were in the thick of it from the outset and seemed to be in an endless period of frantic activity.

There were constant patrols, refuelling, rearming and servicing and repairing of aircraft. The pilots and ground crew were all almost exhausted, but this was a time of kill or be killed. In the first week of the battle, Richthofen claimed seven more victories, the first on 2 April: a BE2d followed by a Sopwith 1½ Strutter of No.43 Squadron, RFC later the same day. Five more followed by the end of the week.

The Albatros aircraft was causing some concerns amongst its pilots, after Vizefeldwebel Festner's Albatros D.III suffered a collapsed port lower wing at 13,000 feet.

With a great deal of luck and skilful airmanship, he managed to get the aircraft down on the ground in one piece. Manfred von Richthofen and his engineering officer examined the aircraft carefully, as this was not the first time there had been reports of a structural failure on the Albatros. A very strongly worded letter was sent to Albatros Company about the problem, and the fact that nothing seemed to be happening about finding the cause. Albatros replied saying that they were in production of the

THE RED BARON

The entire ground crew of Jasta 11 pose for a photograph.

Generalleutnant von Hoeppner being introduced to members of Jasta 11 by Manfred von Richthofen. L–R: Manfred von Richthofen, Generalleutnant Hoeppner, Leutnant Lothar Hartmann, Leutnant Konstatin Krefft, Leutnant Otto Brauneck. Leutnant Hans Kintsch and Leutnant Maximilian Sorg.

CHAPTER ONE

Albatros D.V with a newly designed fuselage, but never addressed the structural failure. This attitude angered Manfred von Richthofen, as he knew that the British were now producing faster and more manoeuvrable aircraft and that German manufacturers were quickly falling behind.

Manfred von Richthofen with some of Jasta 11 pilots. L–R: Leutnant Otto Hartmann, Leutnant Gunther Plueschow, Leutnant Konstatin Krefft, Leutnant Gerog Simon, Leutnant Kurt Wolff, Leutnant Karl Esser, Manfred von Richthofen, Leutnant Hans Hintsch, Leutnant Otto Brauneck, Leutnant Matthof and Leutnant Karl Allmenroder.

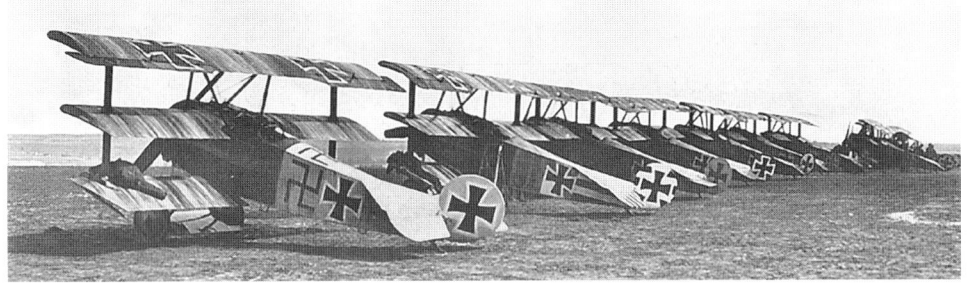

Fokker Dr.I Triplanes of Jasta 11 at Lechelle. All the aircraft have pre-March 1917 Iron Crosses and coloured rudders and the nearest to the camera has a swastika painted on the fuselage. There is no information available to identify these aircraft especially the one with the swastika.

THE RED BARON

Manfred von Richthofen with fellow Jasta 11 pilots. L–R: Leutnant Kurt Wusthoff, Leutnant Wilhelm Reinhard, Richthofen, Unknown, Leutnant Lothar von Richthofen.

Manfred von Richthofen introducing Hauptmann Hellmuth Wilberg to members of Jasta 11. L–R: Hauptmann Reinhard, Oberleutnant Scheffer, Oberleutnant Lothar von Richthofen, Leutnant Groos, Leutnant Mohnicke, Oberleutnant Löwenhardt (behind Wilberg), Leutnant Meyer, Leutnant Muller? Leutnant Von der Osten and Oberleutnant Gerstenberg, Standing behind Manfred von Richthofen is Oberleutnant Bodenshatz JG1 adjutant.

CHAPTER ONE

Above and below: Pilots of Jasta 11 whilst at Roucourt in April 1917. L–R: Vizefeldwebel Festner, Leutnant Schäfer, Manfred von Richthofen, Lothar von Richthofen and Leutnant Kurt Wolff.

Using his influence, Manfred arranged to have his younger brother Lothar join Jasta 11. Although they had their differences, Manfred felt that now he had a close confidant and someone he could trust completely.

Above left: Manfred and Lothar von Richthofen dressed in warm flying kit.

Above right: Manfred von Richthofen arm in arm with his younger brother Lothar.

Left: Manfred von Richthofen with his brother Lothar at Avesnes standing beside his Fokker Dr.I.

CHAPTER ONE

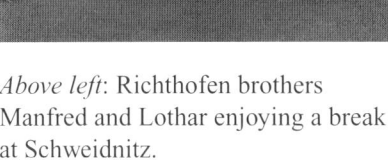

Above left: Richthofen brothers Manfred and Lothar enjoying a break at Schweidnitz.

Above right: Two serious looking brothers, Manfred and Lothar von Richthofen posing for a Sanke postcard picture.

Right: Manfred and Lothar von Richthofen visiting a wounded colleague in hospital. The colleague is said to be Leutnant Victor Shwerk.

THE RED BARON

Lothar and Manfred von Richthofen visiting with colleagues Leutnants von der Osten, Esser and Steinhauser.

Manfred von Richthofen with members of Jasta 11. L–R: Leutnant Hans Weiss, Leutnant Lothar von Richthofen, Leutnant Eberhard Monike, Oberleutnant Wilhelm Haehnelt and Manfred von Richthofen.

CHAPTER ONE

Manfred von Richthofen with his father Albercht von Richthofen on the steps of Chateau Roucourt with members of Jasta 11

Chapter Two

As the months went by, Manfred von Richthofen edged ever closer to the forty victories mark set by Oswald Boelcke, but Jasta 11 was having its share of casualties. Leutnant Eduard Lübbert was shot down and taken prisoner on 30 March. Up to this point it was remarkable that Jasta 11 had only lost two pilots whilst under the command and tutelage of Manfred von Richthofen, and one of those was due to a structural wing failure.

On 11 April, Richthofen equalled Oswald Boelcke's score of forty victories when he shot down a BE.2c from No.13 Squadron, RFC. Two days later, Richthofen shot down three more aircraft, making him the highest-scoring fighter pilot in the German Air Service. By the end of April he had fifty-two 'kills' to his credit, but he was aware that his younger brother,

Above left: Pilots of Jasta 11 at Epinoy airfield. L–R: Manfred von Richthofen, Leutnant Krefft, Lothar von Richthofen and one unknown pilot.

Above right: Manfred von Richthofen with his friend and former Uhlan officer Leutnant Alfred Gerstenberg.

CHAPTER TWO

Lothar was quietly catching up, having downed twenty enemy aircraft in his first month of combat at the Front.

Meanwhile, the German propaganda machine was concerned about losing its star attraction and it was suggested that he might benefit from some well-earned leave, in order to meet the public. To celebrate Manfred's twenty-fifth birthday, he was invited to Berlin to meet the Kaiser. He was flown to Berlin in a DFW.C.V piloted by Leutnant Krefft, who was also going on leave. On arrival, he was invited to a public reception and met with General von Hoeppner, who commanded the German Air Service. On meeting the Kaiser he was given a bust of the emperor as a gift. He also met and dined with Field Marshal von Hindenberg and General Erich Ludendorff.

The following day he flew with Leutnant Krefft in the DFW. C.V to Bad Homburg to meet the Kaiserin.

With all the official formalities over, Manfred von Richthofen headed home to Schweidnitz for a family reunion.

A formally dressed Manfred von Richthofen with his brother Lothar von Richthofen to his right with unknown senior officers.

THE RED BARON

Left: Manfred von Richthofen meeting in Berlin with Oberleutnant Thomsen and Generalleutnant von Hoeppner.

Below: Rittmeister Freiherr Manfred von Richthofen talking with the Kaiserin whilst on a visit to Bad Homberg on 3 May 1917.

CHAPTER TWO

Manfred von Richthofen on far side of fuselage together with Leutnant Fritz Falkenhayn accompanied by the Forbenbeck-Gablenz sisters whilst on a visit to Bad Homberg to meet the Kaiserin.

Manfred von Richthofen looking up at his friend von Falkenhayn standing on the wing of an Aviatik C.II whilst at Bad Homberg for the visit of the Kaiserin.

Another view of Manfred von Richthofen and Leutnant Konstantin Krefft in their Rumpler C.I whilst on a stopover flight to Berlin.

Manfred von Richthofen clambering into Rumpler C.I together with Leutnant Konstatin Krefft after a stopover in Cologne whilst they were on their way to Germany.

CHAPTER TWO

Manfred von Richthofen and Kurt Wolff in the rear seat of a Rumpler C.I flown by Oberleutnant Henning Krefft on their way to Schwerin-Gorries.

Another shot of Richthofen and Wolff in a Rumpler C.I being flown by Krefft.

Manfred von Richthofen and Kurt Wolff preparing to leave Schwerin-Gorries in their converted Rumpler C.I. The rear cockpit had the gun ring removed so that the two of them could squeeze in.

Manfred von Richthofen in flying kit, talking with fellow officer. The Rumpler C.I flown by Leutnant Krefft is being prepared for take-off.

CHAPTER TWO

Manfred von Richthofen seen here with his mother, his sister Ilse and his brother Bolko.

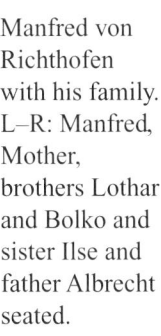

Manfred von Richthofen with his family. L–R: Manfred, Mother, brothers Lothar and Bolko and sister Ilse and father Albrecht seated.

THE RED BARON

Whilst he was away, Jasta 11 was placed in the capable hands of his brother, Leutnant Lothar von Richthofen. In May, Leutnant Hans Hinch was shot down and taken prisoner. In the meantime, Manfred von Richthofen was recalled from leave and ordered to organise four Jagdstaffelns, Nos. 4, 6, 10 and 11, into a single Jagdgeschwader (Wing), which would operate as a single unit. The British later dubbed this as 'Richthofen's Flying Circus'.

Albatros D.V fighters of Jasta 11 ready for action.

Manfred von Richthofen in a Jasta 11 Albatros D.V at Moorseele in February is accompanied by an unidentified pilot from Fl. Abtl. 333

CHAPTER TWO

Richthofen's Fokker Dr.I Triplane.

One of the reasons for this was that Richthofen allowed his pilots to decorate their aircraft in various colours, making it easier to identify each other in combat. Richthofen's Albatros D.V was painted red and it was this all over red painting of his Albatros, and later his Fokker Dr.I Triplane that gave rise to him being referred to as the Red Baron. Another reason for the nickname Flying Circus was that the Wing was constantly striking its tents and moving around, much like a circus.

Suddenly the ground offensive shifted northwards, leaving the sector patrolled by Jasta 11 very quiet; even so, Manfred still managed to increase his tally by shooting down an RE.8 and a SPAD. On 24 June he was officially confirmed as the commander of Jagdgeschwader 1 (JG.1). Realising he couldn't command each Jasta, he immediately appointed Leutnant Kurt Wolff as CO of Jasta 11, Oberleutnant von Doring as CO of Jasta 4, Oberleutnant von Dostler as CO Jasta 6 and Oberleutnant Ernst Freiherr von Althaus as CO Jasta 10 with Oberleutnant Karl Bodenshatz as Adjutant.

Leutnant Kurt Wolff with Manfred von Richthofen in the courtyard of Schloss Roucourt in April 1917.

Left: Manfred von Richthofen with Leutnant Kurt Wolff being chauffeured during a visit to another Jasta.

Below: Manfred von Richthofen at Awoingt in March 1918. L–R: Leutnant August Auer, Leutnant Bender, Leutnant Heldman, Leutnant Grassman, Oberleutnant Erich Lowenhardt, Oberleutnant Karl Bodenschatz, Leutnants Albert Kühn, Manfred von Richthofen (barely recognisable), Oberleutnant Karl Emil Schäfer,

Manfred von Richthofen talking with Leutnant Kurt Wolff.

CHAPTER TWO

Despite being the leader of JG.1, Manfred von Richthofen continued to fly as a fighter pilot. JG.1 suffered its first casualty on 27 June when Leutnant Karl Allmenröder was shot down and taken prisoner.

On July 6 1917, Manfred von Richthofen took off with Jasta 11 on a patrol and ran into six FE.2ds from 20 Squadron, RFC. As they attacked, another Jasta

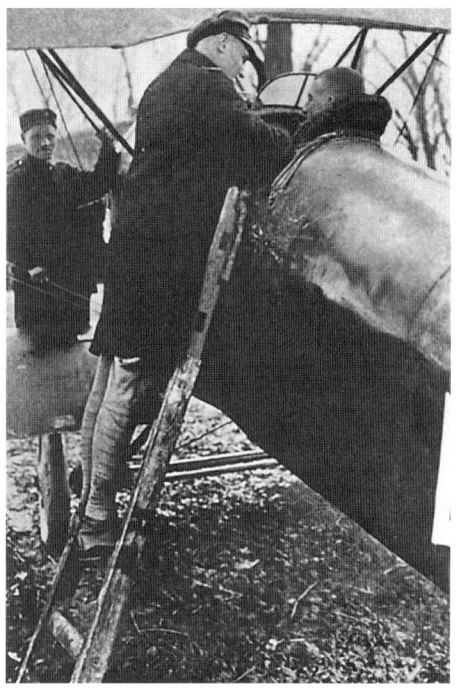

Right: Leutnant Karl Allmenröder talking to Lothar von Richthofen, who is sitting in the cockpit of Manfred's Albatros D.III.

Below: Jasta 11 pilots at Roucourt in April 1917. L–R: Leutnants Allmenroder, Hintsch, Festner, Schiffer, Kurt Wolff, Simon and Brauneck. Seated: Esser, Krefft and Lothar von Richthofen. Manfred von Richthofen is seated in the cockpit of his all red Albatros D.III which was undergoing repairs at the time.

joined them and soon the sky was a mass of milling aircraft. The arrival of four Sopwith Triplanes from No.10 (Naval) Squadron, RNAS put pressure on the Germans. Suddenly a FE.2d closed on Manfred von Richthofen's red Albatros and from a distance, raked it with machine-gun fire. One of the bullets struck Richthofen in the head, gouging a finger-length groove in his skull; others ruptured his fuel line and shattered one of the struts in his lower wing. Richthofen felt the blow to his head and felt his limbs collapse until he was unable to move and suddenly he was blind.

As his aircraft plunged towards the ground, he struggled to regain the use of his limbs and automatically shut the engine off. Wrestling to maintain some semblance of control, he pulled the aircraft out of the dive at about 5,000 feet, still not knowing in which direction he was headed. Then gradually he regained some sight, enough for him to discern the ground beneath him. Picking an empty piece of ground between the shell holes he managed to carry out a forced landing.

As he was clambering out of the wreckage, Leutnant Schroeder, who had seen his crash through a telescope, arrived and took care of him. In the sky above, members of Jasta 11 circled the crash scene in case a British aircraft came in to strafe the site. Manfred von Richthofen was rushed to St Nicholas's Hospital in Courtrai to undergo surgery.

Manfred von Richthofen's Albatros D.V having carried out an emergency landing in a field.

CHAPTER TWO

Manfred von Richthofen's Albatros D.V in a field after he had carried out an emergency landing after receiving a head wound.

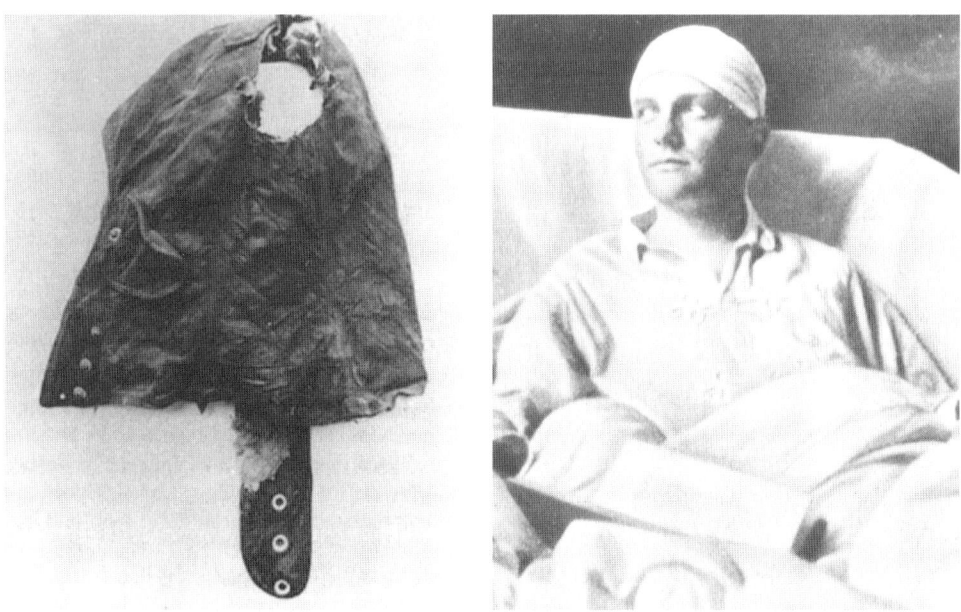

Above left: Richthofen's flying helmet showing the hole where he was hit by a bullet.

Above right: Manfred von Richthofen in his hospital bed after surgery.

Above: Rare, but not a good quality, photograph of Manfred von Richthofen with his brother Lothar von Richthofen, both wearing their full medal bars. Manfred still has his head bandaged from the head wound he received during a dogfight.

Left: Albrecht von Richthofen visiting his son Manfred in hospital recovering from a head wound

CHAPTER TWO

Above left: Manfred von Richthofen with his nurse Katie Otersdorf.

Above right: Side view of Manfred von Richthofen whilst recovering from his head wound.

Oberleutnant Edward Dostler wearing Manfred von Richthofen's Pour Le Mérite after being told that he was to be awarded the honour later. Manfred von Richthofen was making a visit to Jasta 6 whilst recovering from the head wound, as can be seen in the photograph.

THE RED BARON

The incident, which nearly cost Manfred von Richthofen his life, changed his personality. He was never an overfriendly, sociable person, but he became almost a recluse, allowing only family and very close friends to be near him. Tired of the endless visitors that came to visit him, and against orders, he left hospital.

The German High Command decided to keep Richthofen from flying combat missions for a while and sent him on a tour of the various Jastas. Despite the desire to get back into action, Manfred looked forward to seeing some old colleagues and enjoyed the adulation he received. He was also invited to visit the Pfalz factory and the LFG factory to test their new aircraft, Pfalz Dr.I Triplane and the LFG Roland D.III.

On 25 July, Manfred von Richthofen returned to JG.1, taking over command from Oberleutnant von Dostler, who had been temporarily in charge. Richthofen was briefed on the new aircraft that were now available to him and the new aircraft that the enemy had put into the air. Among these was the diminutive Sopwith F1 Camel, which in the hands of a skilled pilot, was a highly manoeuvrable killing machine. Within a couple of months Manfred von Richthofen was back in the air, adding to his tally of victims.

Manfred von Richthofen being visited by members of Jasta 11 whilst in hospital.

CHAPTER TWO

Manfred von Richthofen paying a visit to a training camp near Cologne. The unknown officer with the flight gear on was accompanying Richthofen on the trip.

Manfred von Richthofen with Leutnant Konstantin Krefft about to leave for a 'hunting' trip.

THE RED BARON

Manfred von Richthofen in his Albatros D.V of Jasta 11 prepares to depart a wet soggy airfield.

A relaxed Manfred von Richthofen visiting Jasta 5 with von Hippel, Oberleutnant Richard Flashar, unknown, Leutnant Schloemer and Leutnant Wilhelm Lehmann.

Manfred von Richthofen about to leave Jasta 5 in his Albatros D.V. Behind Richthofen is Oberleutnant Richard Flashar, Leutnant Wilhelm Lehmann and Leutnant Schaumberg.

CHAPTER TWO

Manfred von Richthofen in conversation with Leutnant Alfred Gerstenberg in front of Richthofen's Halberstadt D.

Manfred von Richthofen talking with Oberleutnant Richard Flashar whilst on a visit to Jasta 5 at Bertincourt.

THE RED BARON

Manfred von Richthofen being dressed for a flight after a stopover at Cologne.

Manfred von Richthofen chatting with Hauptmann Spranger CO of Cologne.

CHAPTER TWO

Right: Manfred von Richthofen chatting with Leutnant Alfred Muller during a stopover in Moorseele.

Below: Manfred von Richthofen about to test a Roland D.III

Left: Manfred von Richthofen deep in conversation with Oberleutnant Hans Bethge.

Below: Manfred von Richthofen visiting II Marine Flieger Abteilung in his Albatros D.III.

CHAPTER TWO

Above: Manfred von Richthofen visiting II Marine Flieger Abteilung, with a sailor enjoying a moment sitting in the cockpit of Richthofen's Albatros D.V.

Right: Manfred von Richthofen in the cockpit of a Pfalz Dr.1 triplane whilst on a visit to Speyer to test the aircraft.

Manfred von Richthofen in the cockpit of a Pfalz Dr.1 prototype with Pfalz test pilot Ernst Schlegel behind Richthofen and Alfred Everbusch founder of the Pfalz Company, leaning into the cockpit.

Manfred von Richthofen visiting the Pfalz facility at Speyer. L–R: Leutnant Auer, Ernst Everbusch (co-owner), Hauptmann Willy Meyer, Hauptmann Albert Mühlig-Hofmann (Idflieg), Leutnant Konstatin Krefft, Manfred von Richthofen, Oberleutnant Fritz von Falkenhayn, Oberleutnant Adolf Ritter von Tutschek, Ernst Schlegel (test engineer), Alfred Eversbusch (co-owner) and unknown.

CHAPTER TWO

Manfred von Richthofen taking off in his Albatros D.V.

Manfred von Richthofen boarding his Albatros D.III after a visit to an unknown Jasta.

Manfred von Richthofen visiting Jasta 5 and returning the salute of Leutnant Fritz Rumey. Oberleutnant Richard Flashar is standing behind Richthofen with Leutnant Wilhelm Lehmann and Leutnant Schaumberg to his right.

Manfred von Richthofen in an LFG Roland at the Roland Works.

CHAPTER TWO

Above: Manfred von Richthofen with some Austro-Hungarian pilots at one of their airfields whilst on a visit.

Right: Manfred von Richthofen on a visit to a flying school. The identity of the other two men is not known.

Above: Manfred von Richthofen studying a map whilst on a visit to a training camp.

Left: Manfred von Richthofen with Hauptmann Otto Zimmer at Vorhaus.

CHAPTER TWO

Above: Manfred von Richthofen arriving in Flanders in his Albatros D.V.

Right: A very relaxed looking Manfred von Richthofen.

But his actions in the air gave some cause for concern that he was still suffering from the effects of the head wound, as he became more intent on closing with the enemy to almost touching distance before opening fire. While all this was going on, a parade for the Kaiser was held on the airfield at Courtrai.

Left: The Kaiser taking Rittmeister Manfred von Richthofen's salute at a parade in August 1917. Richthofen's bandaged head is very apparent.

Below: Manfred von Richthofen with other officers at the Kaiser's parade. Richthofen can be seen striding towards the camera, with Berthold to his left and Oberleutnants Edward Dostler, Kranth and Baur to his right.

CHAPTER TWO

Manfred von Richthofen waiting for the Kaiser's parade to start.

Standing in line awaiting the arrival of the Kaiser and wearing their Pour Le Mérite awards L–R: Manfred von Richthofen, von Pechman, Oberleutnant Edwards Dostler and Berthold.

Left: Manfred von Richthofen in conversation with Hauptmann Wilberg of Koft.4. The identity of the other two officers is not known.

Below: Officers casually awaiting the arrival of the Kaiser.

CHAPTER TWO

Above: The Kaiser's parade with Manfred von Richthofen in front giving the salute.

Right: Manfred von Richthofen at the Kaiser's parade, the bandage around his head can just be seen below his cap.

Pilots of Jasta 11 being introduced to General der Infantrie Erich von Ludendorff by Manfred von Richthofen. Richthofen's Albatros D.V can be seen in the background with a ladder against the fuselage.

Senior officers of Jasta 11 talking with General der Infantrie Erich von Ludendorff and his party after their meeting with Jasta 11 pilots.

CHAPTER TWO

The first of the Fokker Dr.I Triplanes arrived at Courtrai at the end of August, and the work of training the pilots to fly the Triplane began.

In the meantime, Richthofen had increased his tally to fifty-nine when he shot down a RE.2. Two days later, in his first combat flight in the Fokker Triplane, he shot down a RE.8. His sixty-first victim was a Sopwith Pup flown by Lieutenant A.F. Bird, whom he encountered just after the Sopwith Pup had crashed into a tree.

The red Fokker Dr.I belonging to Rittmeister Manfred von Richthofen under armed guard possibly because it was close to the front line.

Aerial shot of Courtrai taken in July 1917. In the upper left-hand corner can be seen the airfield of Jasta 4 and Jasta 11 at Marckbeke.

THE RED BARON

Lieutenant A.F. Bird, of 46 Squadron, RFC together with his adversary Manfred von Richthofen on 3 November 1917 after being shot down by the latter for his 61st victory.

Another shot of Lieutenant. A.F.Bird of 46 Squadron, RFC after being shot down by Manfred von Richthofen for his 61st victory.

CHAPTER TWO

Manfred von Richthofen and Anthony Fokker with one of Richthofen's victims, a Sopwith Pup B1795.

Manfred von Richthofen with Leutnant Eberhard Mohnike at the crash site of his latest victim, a Sopwith Pup B1795.

THE RED BARON

Manfred von Richthofen with Leutnant Ebergard Mohnike at the crash site of Richthofen's latest victim, Lieutenant A.F. Bird's Sopwith Pup.

Manfred von Richthofen with his brother Lothar and father Albrecht.

CHAPTER TWO

Manfred von Richthofen (far left in front row) attending the funeral of Leutnant Wilhelm Gürke of Jasta 5.

Manfred von Richthofen was still having problems with his head wound and so concerned with his health were the German High Command, that at the beginning of September 1917 he was sent on a long leave of convalescence, leaving JG.1 in the hands of his brother Lothar.

That same month, Jasta 10 suffered a great loss when Leutnant Werner Voss was shot down and killed.

Voss had only arrived at the beginning of August with thirty-three victories to his credit, and within a twenty-one day period had shot down another ten enemy aircraft. When he died on 23 September he had just scored his forty-eighth 'kill' before falling to the guns of an SE.5. Jasta 11 also suffered a major loss when their leader, Leutnant Kurt Wolff, was shot down and killed.

These losses were kept from Manfred von Richthofen until he returned to JG.1 on 23 October.

When new aircraft were designed and built, the manufacturers would have their company test pilots fly the aircraft at shows, before inviting some of the military pilots to fly them. It was known that certain aircraft manufacturers offered some of these pilots monetary inducements to favourably endorse their aircraft. Richthofen, was well aware of this practice

Above left: Leutnant Werner Voss and Manfred von Richthofen deep in conversation.

Above right: Leutnant Werner Voss and Manfred von Richthofen.

Manfred von Richthofen meeting with fellow pilots. On his right is Leutnant Kurt Wolff.

CHAPTER TWO

Fokker Dr.I Triplane of Jasta 11.

and refused point blank to have anything to do with it. He recognised that by accepting and endorsing these aircraft, pilots could be endangering the lives of other pilots, as well as their own, if the aircraft was not up to the required standard. There is no doubt that his thoughts on this type of practice were relayed to all the pilots in JG.1 and strict warnings issued should anyone become involved.

The Fokker Dr.I Triplane in the hands of a highly skilled pilot was almost the ultimate killing machine, but in the hands of an ordinary pilot it was an unforgiving aircraft. Not long after Richthofen's return to JG.1, some problems arose with the plane. Leutnant Heinrich Gontermann was killed when in the process of diving on an enemy aircraft; the top wing of his aircraft suffered a major structural failure and broke free. Two days later, Leutnant Pastor from Jasta 11 died when his aircraft suffered a similar structural failure. Richthofen and his engineering officer Leutnant Krefft, then carried out a detailed examination of the remaining Fokker Dr.I Triplanes in JG.1 and found numerous faults and examples of shoddy workmanship.

An incensed Manfred von Richthofen contacted Anthony Fokker and insisted that all the faults were to be rectified before he would allow any of his pilots to fly in the aircraft again.

Manfred von Richthofen talking to German Chancellor Georg Michaelis whilst waiting for the arrival of the new Fokker Triplane.

Front three-quarter view of the Fokker Triplane at Marckbeke in August 1917.

CHAPTER TWO

Anthony Fokker talking with General Sixt von Arnim about the Fokker Triplane.

Manfred von Richthofen and Chancellor Georg Michaelis about to watch a demonstration of his Fokker Triplane.

Close-up shot of Anthony Fokker in the cockpit of his Fokker Triplane about to carry out a demonstration with General von Lossberg and Manfred von Richthofen close to the fuselage.

Anthony Fokker about to demonstrate his Fokker Triplane. Seen here talking with Major General von Lossberg. Behind is Manfred von Richthofen listening intently to what is being discussed.

CHAPTER TWO

Manfred von Richthofen and Chancellor Georg Michaelis watching Anthony Fokker put his Fokker Triplane through its paces.

Manfred von Richthofen talking with Chancellor Georg Michaelis.

THE RED BARON

Anthony Fokker in flying clothes talking with General Sixt von Arnim, with Chancellor Georg Michaelis on the left and a smiling Manfred von Richthofen behind.

Chancellor Georg Michaelis talking with Anthony Fokker [in civilian clothes] after his demonstration flight.

CHAPTER TWO

Chancellor Georg Michaelis, General Sixt von Arnim and Manfred von Richthofen at Marckbeke in August 1917 at the demonstration of the Fokker Triplane.

Oberleutnant Henning Krefft, Anthony Fokker, Leutnant Kurt Wolff and Manfred von Richthofen at Schwerin-Gorries in March 1917.

Manfred von Richthofen and Anthony Fokker in his car.

Anthony Fokker and Manfred von Richthofen with two unknown officers both wearing observers' badges on their jackets at Schwerin-Gorries.

CHAPTER TWO

But aviation was gaining pace and the Fokker Dr.I Triplane was now considered to be obsolete, its place taken by the Fokker D.VII. Richthofen wasn't impressed, so went back to flying his old Albatros D.V. and in the following two weeks added a D.H.5 and a S.E.5a to his tally.

There has always been a question over some of the claims of 'kills' by Richthofen. In the earlier years any claim had to be supported by a third party, but as Richthofen's fame increased, his word was considered to be enough. In the case of the SE.5a in Richthofen's report on 7 April 1918, he had stated that he opened fire on the aircraft from a distance of 200 metres. This was very unusual, as Richthofen was known to go to almost 'touching' distance before opening fire. He also stated that after firing at the aircraft it almost disintegrated. Research has found that the aircraft in question was shot down, but not until the 8 April and much further north of where Richthofen was flying. Another claim made on 7 April was for a

Albatros D.III belonging to Manfred von Richthofen.

Rare photograph of Manfred von Richthofen taking off in his all-red Albatros D.V.

JG 1 at Lechelle in April 1918.

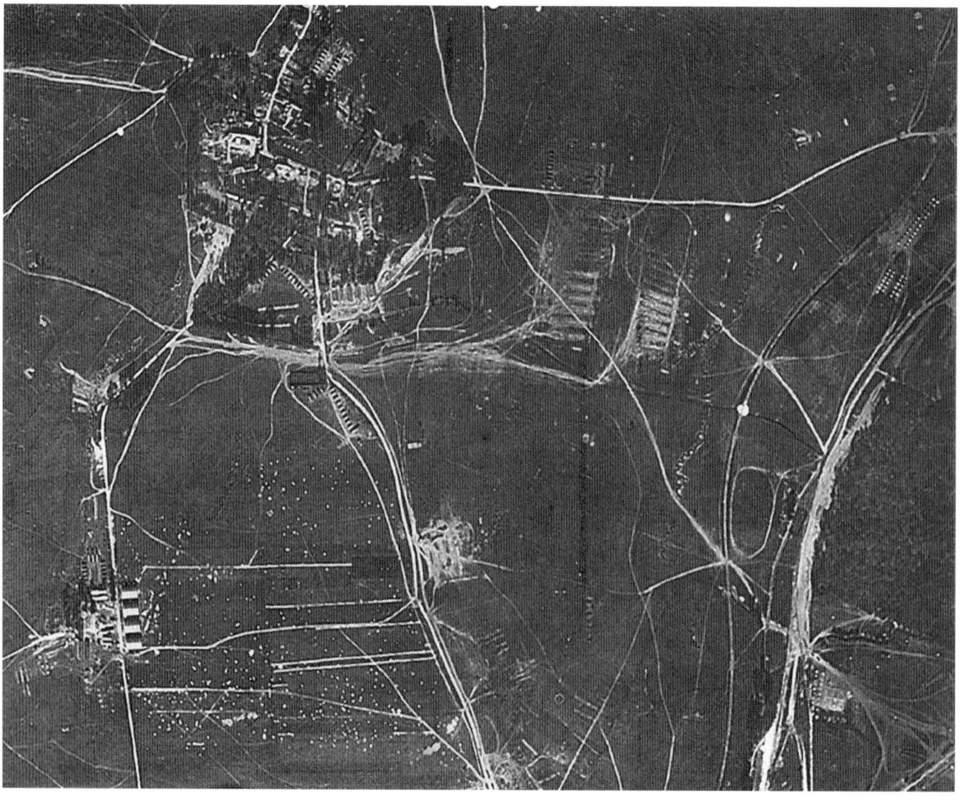

Aerial shot of the airfield at Lechelle.

CHAPTER TWO

Lechelle April 1918. L–R: Wolfram von Richthofen, Leutnant Scholtz, Leutnant Kariuss, Leutnant Joachim Wolff, Leutnant Sigfried Lischke, Manfred von Richthofen, Oberleutnant Erich Lowenhardt, Leutnant Werner Steinhauser and Leutnant Hans Weiss. Note the ones wearing parachute harness.

SPAD single-seat scout, but there were no SPADS flying that day and the only allied aircraft shot down was a Nieuport 27 and that was in the late evening.

In the March of 1918, the Germans had made a major push on the Western Front in an effort to break through the stalemate that had reduced the war to trench warfare. During the following six weeks, Manfred von Richthofen is said to have shot down a further seventeen aircraft taking his tally to eighty. The last was a Sopwith Camel of 3 Squadron RAF flown by 2nd Lieutenant D. G. Lewis. (A full list of Richthofen's victories is at the end of the book.)

Richthofen's Flying Circus was living up to its name, as order after order to move was suddenly countermanded by another order, forcing JG.1 to strike their tents at Lechelle, until a final order sent them to Cappy.

The weather didn't help, as torrential rain turned the airfield into a quagmire, but within days the weather had cleared enough for Richthofen to go on patrol with pilots from Jasta 11. Richthofen was back flying with a much-improved Fokker Dr.I Triplane painted in its distinctive red.

On Sunday, 21 April, two three-man Kettes (flight of three aircraft) from Jasta 11 took off from Cappy, led by Leutnant Manfred von Richthofen. With him was his cousin Leutnant Wolfram von Richthofen and Vizefeldwebel Scholz, with Leutnant Reiss leading the second Kette.

On the Allied side, four Sopwith Camels from 209 Squadron, RAF, led by Captain Roy Brown, started to patrol their sector between Hangard and Albert. Two more RAF flights took to the air in five-minute intervals, unknowingly flying on a line parallel with that of Richthofen's flight, but at a different height. One of the Allied flights came into contact with two Albatros D.Vs flying a reconnaissance mission. They attacked, shooting one of them down whilst the other beat a hasty retreat. In the meantime, Jasta 5 had joined up with Richthofen's flight and attacked two RE.8s from No. 3 Squadron AFC, who were carrying out an artillery observation mission over the Front Line.

One of the RE.8s was shot down, but the Fokker Dr.I Triplanes of Jasta 5 had drifted over the British lines and were suddenly subjected to intense

Albatros D.Vs of Jasta 11 whilst with the 4 Armee in Flanders in July 1917. The various wing designs were indicative of the freedom the pilots had to paint their aircraft in such away as to be able to identify them.

CHAPTER TWO

anti-aircraft fire. This drew the attention of the Sopwith Camels from 209 Squadron, who swooped down to attack. One of the Camel pilots was a novice pilot, Lieutenant May, who had been told to stay out of the fight and just observe. He inadvertently got drawn into the fight when a

Albatros D.Vs of Jasta 11 at Roucourt in June 1917. The nearest aircraft to the camera is Manfred von Richthofen's all red Albatros D.V.

Richthofen's Flying Circus Jasta 11.

Left: Albatros D.IIIs of Richthofen's Flying Circus. Manfred von Richthofen's Albatros is the second from the front without the German Cross on the fuselage.

Below: Anthony Fokker's Triplane at Marckbeke in August 1917.

CHAPTER TWO

Said to be the last shot of Manfred von Richthofen as he took off on his last fateful flight.

Fokker Dr.I Triplane, piloted by Leutnant Wolfram von Richthofen, flew past him and he gave pursuit. Realising he was fast losing altitude and that his guns had jammed after a long burst, he headed for the Somme valley and safety.

This incident, however, had been spotted by the eagle eye of Manfred von Richthofen and he went after Lieutenant May's Sopwith Camel. Suddenly May found himself weaving and diving to try and shake off the red Fokker Dr.I Triplane that now had attached itself to his tail. Flying at 3,000 feet, Captain Roy Brown saw the fledgling pilot in trouble and dived to help. As he closed on the all-red Fokker Dr.I Triplane, he opened fire. Richthofen suddenly became aware that he was being pursued, but for some unknown reason ignored this and continued after Lieutenant May's Camel.

Richthofen was ignoring his own rule of flying at ground level over the enemy's front line exposing himself to ground fire. He had told his own pilots on numerous occasions the dangers of doing this, yet he continued on.

THE RED BARON

A view of the Somme valley above Corbie. It was while flying low over the trees that Manfred von Richthofen was killed in front of the clearing on the right of the photograph. The figure in the centre is that of Lieutenant Will Dyson the Australian Official artist. The chateau on the left was used as a dressing station in April 1918.

A view of the Somme valley above Corbie, looking east, where Manfred von Richthofen was killed flying over trees on the ridge on the right.

CHAPTER TWO

Maybe it was the thought of another easy victory that spurred him on, but no one will ever know. Some witnesses said that they saw Richthofen's Fokker Dr.I Triplane hit several times from Roy Brown's guns. Richthofen continued to close on his prey and was now flying at about 50 feet above the ground. Flying along the edge of the Somme, the two aircraft twisted and turned and drew closer to where machine-gun emplacements of the 53rd Battery, Australian Field Artillery, were situated.

Sergeant Cedric Popkin, who was in charge of one of the machine-gun emplacements, watched as the two aircraft hurtled towards him. He saw spurts of flame come from the all-red Fokker Triplane's guns as bullets struck the Sopwith Camel, some of them hitting the ground near the machine-gun positions. As the two aircraft swept past, Gunner Buie and Gunner Evans, on the orders of Sergeant Popkin, opened fire with their machine guns on

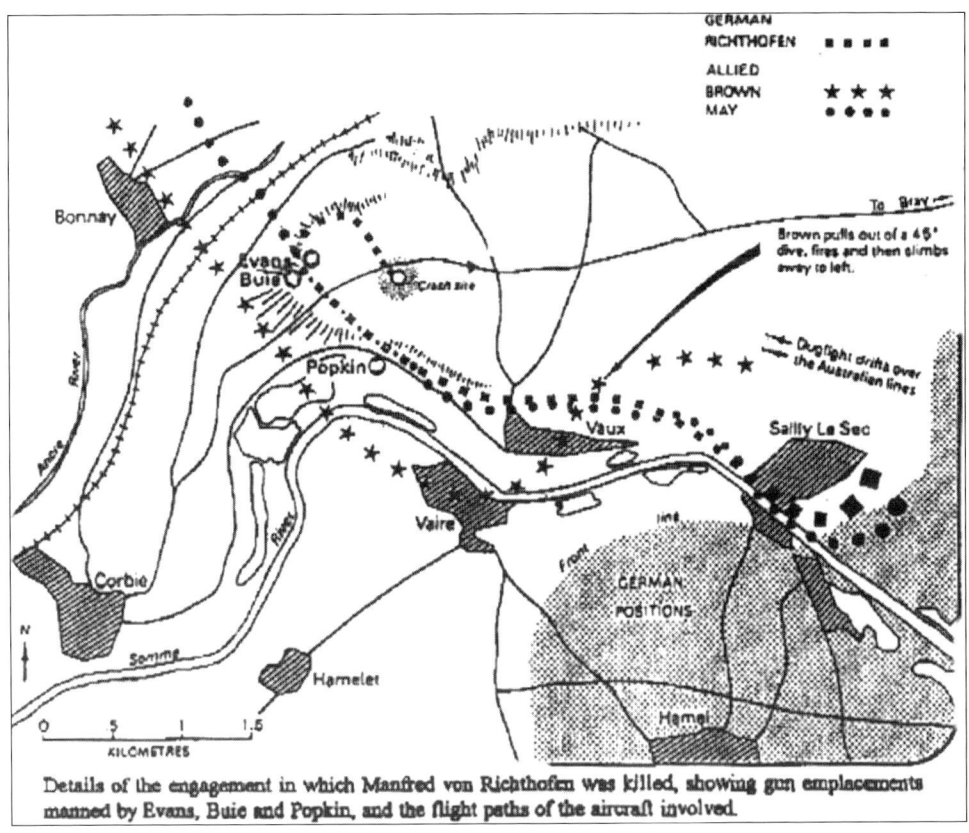

Details of the engagement in which Manfred von Richthofen was killed, showing gun emplacements manned by Evans, Buie and Popkin, and the flight paths of the aircraft involved.

Map showing the engagement of Richthofen's aircraft and the positions of the Australian machine-gun emplacements.

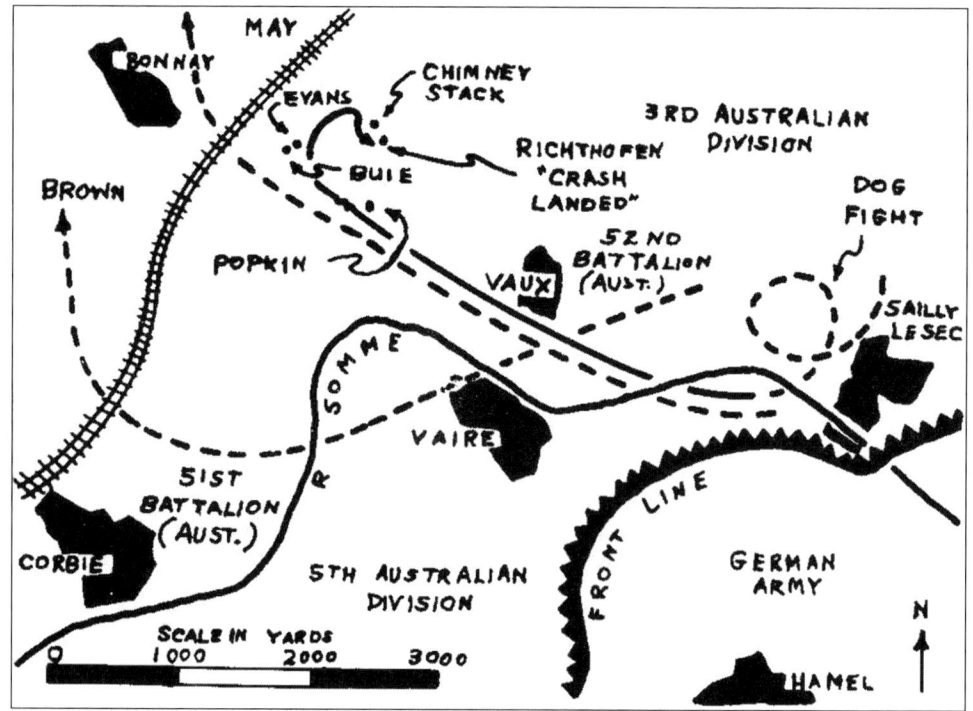

Map showing a closer view of the engagement of Richthofen's Fokker with the Australian gun emplacements.

the all-red Fokker and saw their bullets hit the fuselage. Sergeant Popkin then opened fire as they swept past him.

The Fokker Triplane seemed to shudder momentarily, then side-slipped, dropping even lower. Then it turned as if to come back towards where the machine guns were, before going into a spiral and crashing into a beet field alongside the Bray-Corbie road. The undercarriage was ripped off as the aircraft first bounced then nose-dived into the ground. Richthofen was hurled face-first into the butts of his twin machine guns, causing a broken nose and numerous bruises to his face.

His body hung limply over the edge of the cockpit, partially restrained by the loose harness. Within minutes, some of the Australian Gunners arrived at the scene. Word was quickly sent back to headquarters that the Red Baron had been shot down and was dead.

Orders were quickly issued for a salvage party to go and retrieve the pilot's body, to salvage what was left of the aircraft and place a guard on it.

CHAPTER TWO

Australian machine gun crew that brought down Manfred von Richthofen's Fokker Dr.I Triplane with Sergeant Cedric B. Popkin at the trigger handles.

No. 24 Machine Gun Company, the men that shot down the Red Baron Rittmeister Freiherr Manfred von Richthofen.

One of your AA machine guns brought down in J19 B pilot Capt. VON. RICHTHOFEN aaa Congratulations.

CHAPTER TWO

Painting depicting the removal of Manfred von Richthofen's body from the wreckage of his Fokker Dr.I Triplane by Australian troops.

When word got around that the pilot was the famous Rittmeister Manfred von Richthofen – The Red Baron – souvenir hunters almost stripped the aircraft.

Richthofen's body was taken to No.3 Hangar of the Australian Flying Corps at Poulainville, where it was subjected to a cursory examination.

They found a single bullet wound passing from right to left, entering from just beneath the right armpit and exiting one half-inch above the left nipple, having been deflected after hitting the spine.

Various medical officers subjected Manfred von Richthofen's body to a series of 'post-mortems'. They differ in many ways, but the consensus of opinion is that Richthofen was struck by a single bullet fired from below. But who fired the fatal bullet that killed the Red Baron has always been a bone of contention. There can only be four possible answers.

Opposite: British signal from General Rawlinson to 5th Australian Division stating that the German aircraft they shot down was that of Manfred von Richthofen.

THE RED BARON

AFC pilots looking at the wreckage of the Red Baron's Fokker Triplane.

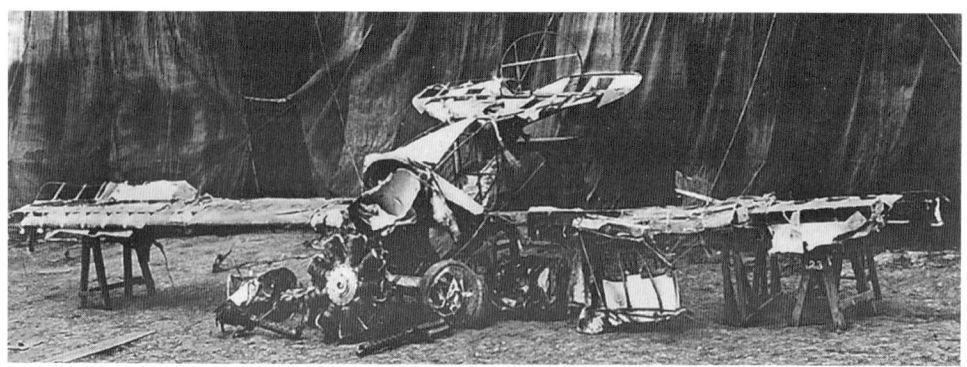

Above: Remains of Richthofen's Fokker Dr.I Triplane collected after his crash.

Opposite above: AFC pilots examining the wreckage of the Red Baron's Fokker Dr.I Triplane.

Opposite below: AFC pilots examining the guns from Manfred von Richthofen's Fokker Dr.I Triplane.

CHAPTER TWO

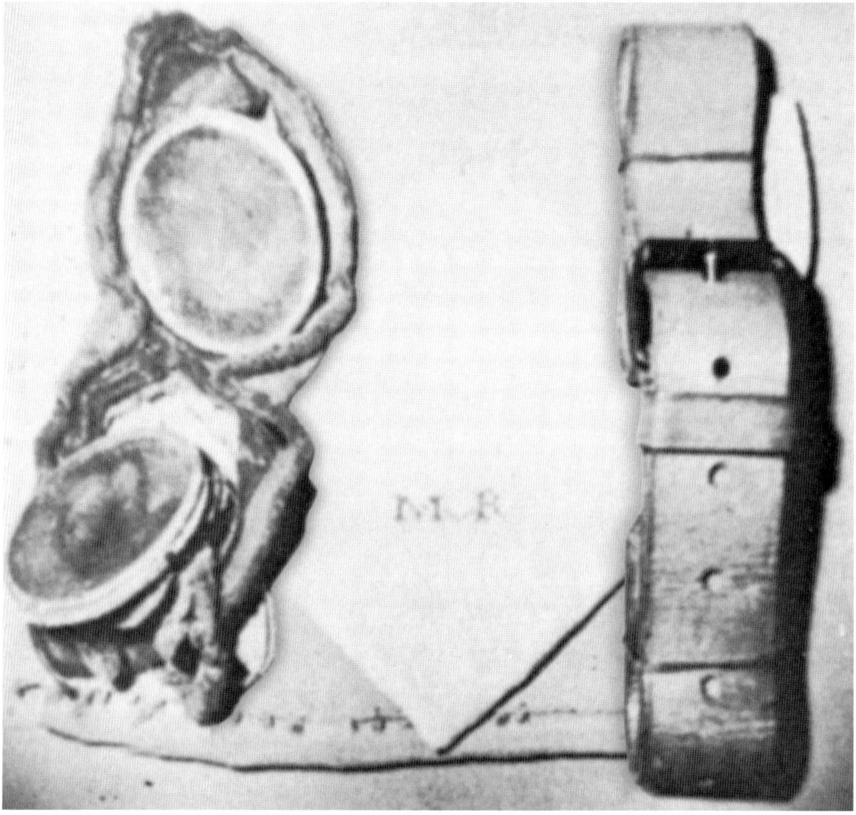

THE RED BARON

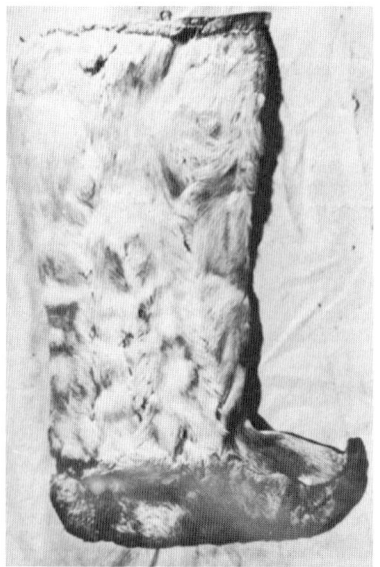

Above: Manfred von Richthofen's goggles and belt recovered from his body.

Left: One of Manfred von Richthofen's boots recovered fro the crash site.

CHAPTER TWO

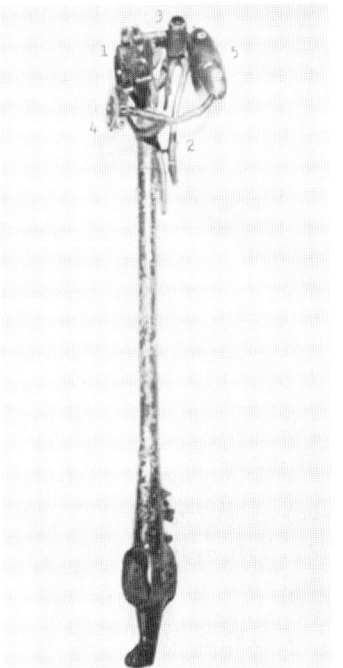

Right: Control Column recovered from the wreckage of Richthofen's Fokker Dr.I Triplane.

Below: Drawing depicting Manfred von Richthofen's body after being recovered from his crashed aircraft. Australian officers showing their respect for a fellow aviator.

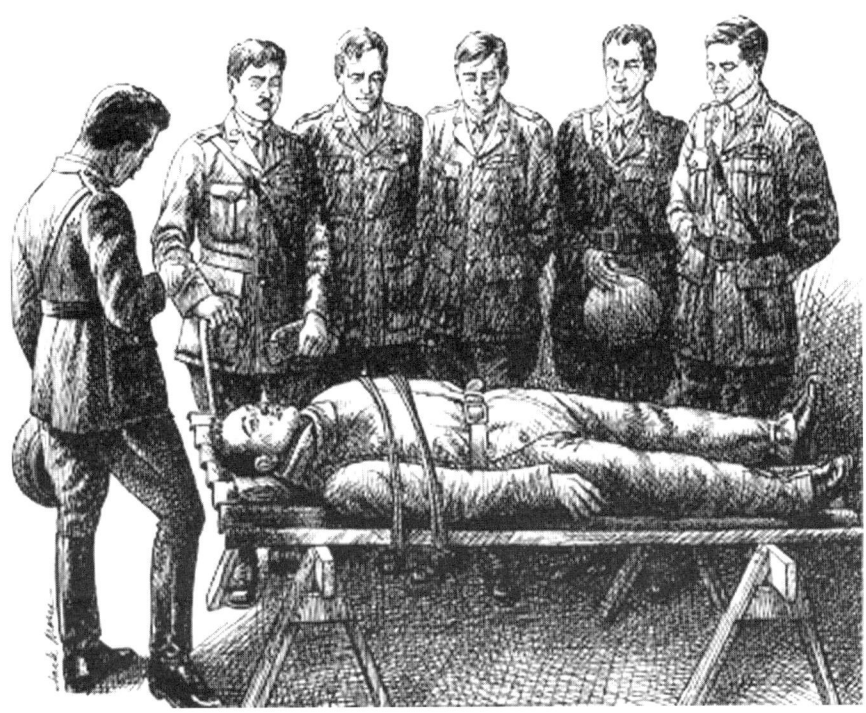

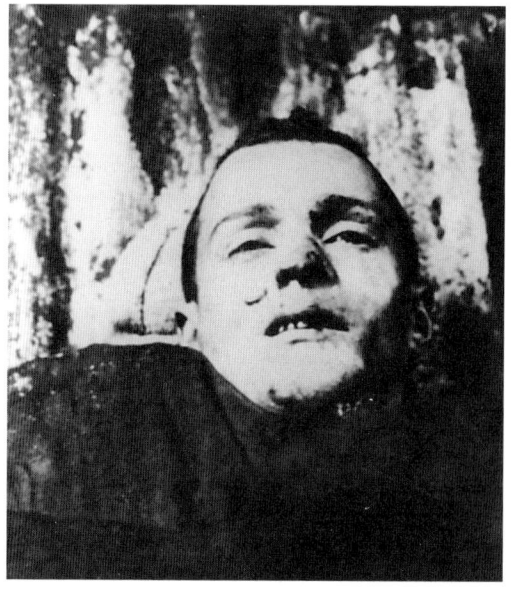
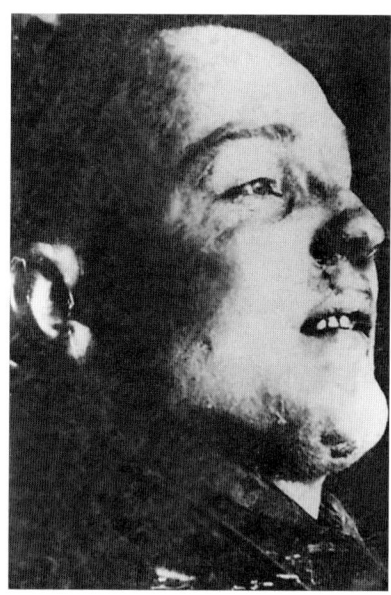

Above left: The battered face of Manfred von Richthofen in death.

Above right: A side view of the battered face of Manfred von Richthofen.

Drawing of the position of Manfred von Richthofen's body when hit by the bullet from the Australian machine-gun crew.

CHAPTER TWO

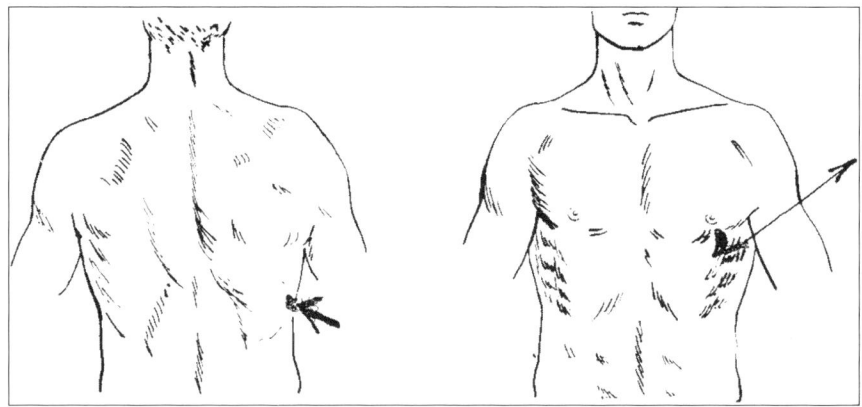

Drawing of Richthofen's torso showing the angle and path of the bullet that killed him.

1. Captain Roy Brown.

The fact that the bullet was fired from below and from the right-hand side has been accepted by almost everybody, and is the main factor that discounts Captain Roy Brown's claim. The .303 single rifle bullet (this bullet was used in the Lee-Enfield rifle, Vickers and Lewis machine guns) entered Richthofen's body underneath his right armpit and exited just above his left nipple. It is accepted that Captain Brown did approach from the right and did open fire on Richthofen's aircraft, but unless Richthofen banked his aircraft sharply to the left at that moment, and Captain Brown never mentioned that in his report, there was no way he could have inflicted such

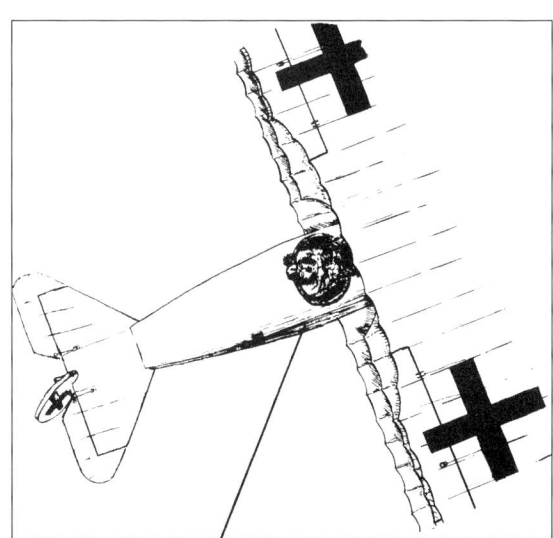

Drawing showing the angle of the aircraft and the bullet's trajectory.

a wound. There were also eyewitness reports that after Captain Brown had been seen to fire on Richthofen, his red Fokker Triplane continued to chase after Lieutenant May, firing its guns. Had Richthofen suffered the fatal wound fired by Captain Brown this could not have happened, as Richthofen would have died almost instantly.

2. Australian Gunner Robert Buie.
The track and angle of the bullet that struck Manfred von Richthofen is crucial. In Buie's statement he said that Richthofen's Fokker was coming towards, and a little to the right of him, when he opened fire from a distance of about 40 yards. There is no evidence that Buie fired at Richthofen from behind.

3. Australian Gunner Sergeant Cedric Popkin.
The most likely candidate for shooting down Manfred von Richthofen was Sergeant Popkin. Popkin was manning a Lewis gun at one of the machine-gun emplacements when Manfred von Richthofen's red Fokker Triplane was spotted on the tail of Lieutenant May's Sopwith Camel. Popkin first opened fire as the two aircraft approached from the direction of the Somme valley, but failed to hit him. Richthofen then came under fire from Gunners Buie and Evans as the Fokker turned away from Popkin. Popkin continued to fire at the retreating Triplane from a distance of around 40 yards, and this is the moment it is likely that the fatal bullet hit Richthofen. One has to wonder why, if out of a long burst of machine-gun fire, only one bullet managed to strike his body.

4. An unknown rifleman
This then leads us to the fourth possibility. Was this a lucky hit by an unknown rifleman? It is accepted that any number of people would have opened fire on the low-flying Fokker Triplane as it came within range. The chances are that we will never know, but the mystery helps to keep alive the legend and story of Rittmeister Freiherr Manfred von Richthofen – The Red Baron.

   Manfred von Richthofen was buried in the small village cemetery at Bertangles with full military honours. The service was carried out by an Anglican chaplain followed by a three-shot salute by twelve Australian soldiers. A cross, made from a four-bladed propeller, was placed at the head of the grave, which was covered in a floral tribute. However, that evening local villagers entered the cemetery and ripped down the cross and destroyed all the flowers, incensed that a German had been buried in their local cemetery.

CHAPTER TWO

Manfred von Richthofen's coffin being carried from the AFC camp.

Manfred von Richthofen's coffin being carried to the open truck.

AFC officers following the pen back truck carrying Richthofen's coffin out of the camp.

Australian Flying Corps leading the funeral cortege with rifles reversed with officers following the coffin-carrying truck.

CHAPTER TWO

Richthofen's coffin being taken to the cemetery with a guard of honour.

Lowering Manfred von Richthofen's coffin into its grave.

Manfred von Richthofen's grave being filled in.

Australian guard of honour preparing to fire a volley of three shots over Richthofen's grave.

CHAPTER TWO

Funeral volley over the grave of the Red Baron, Manfred von Richthofen. Note the number of local villagers present.

Service being conducted by an army chaplain over the grave of Manfred von Richthofen.

THE RED BARON

AFC officers laying wreaths at the grave of Manfred von Richthofen.

Local villagers and members of the Australian Flying Corps looking at the grave of Manfred von Richthofen. Some of those villagers looking on may have been responsible for trying to dig it up that same night, objecting to the burying of a German in their local graveyard at Sailly le Sec, Somme.

CHAPTER TWO

Above: Manfred von Richthofen's grave with a cross made from the remnants of a propeller at the head.

Right: Excellent shot of Manfred von Richthofen's grave showing clearly the cross made out of the remnants of a propeller.

THE RED BARON

Excellent shot of a German Fokker Dr.I Triplane from Jasta 6 looking for Richthofen after he had been reported missing. The photograph was taken by a crew from Flieger Abteilung 17 who were in the process of photographing enemy positions.

The news that Manfred von Richthofen had been shot down and killed stunned the German nation. Initially the news had filtered through to Jagdgeschwader 1 that he had crashed, but had been seen leaving the scene on a hill near Corbie.

The following evening a lone British aircraft dropped canisters containing the message:

> 'Rittmeister von Richthofen was fatally wounded in aerial combat and was buried with full military honours.'

The moment that message was received, the adjutant of Jagdgeschwader 1, Oberleutnant Karl Bodenshatz handed Oberleutnant Wilhelm Reinhard an envelope which held the following message:

> 'In the event that I do not return from a patrol, Oberleutnant Reinhard of Jasta 6 is to command the Geschwader.
>
> Freiherr von Richthofen, Rittmeister.

CHAPTER TWO

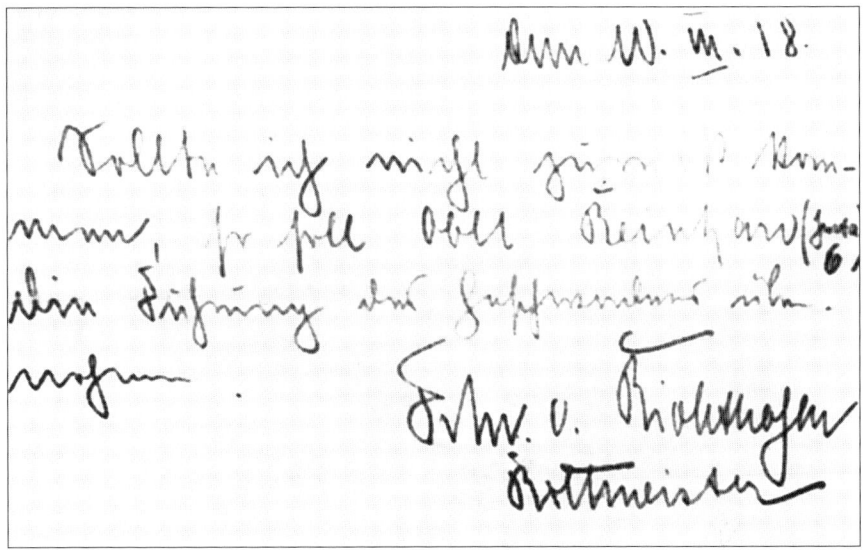

Note written by Manfred von Richthofen giving instructions about who should take command of the Jasta in the event of him being shot down. The note reads: 'In the event that I do not return from a patrol, Oberleutnant Reinhard of Jasta 6 is to command the Geschwader.' It is signed Freiherr von Richthofen, Rittmeister.

After the war, Manfred von Richthofen's remains were moved from the small cemetery at Bertangles to a cemetery at Fricourt. Then in 1925, Manfred von Richthofen's remains were exhumed and taken back to Germany.

The family's intention was for the Great War ace's body to be re-interred in the Schweidnitz cemetery next to the graves of his father Albrecht and his brother Lothar, who had been killed in a post-war air crash in 1922. However, the German Government requested that he should be interred at the Invalidenfriedhof, Berlin, the traditional resting place of the Prussian Army. This was agreed and Richthofen's body received a state funeral. In due course the Nazi authorities held a grandiose memorial ceremony, where his mother and surviving members of Jagdgeschwader 1 were present at the site of the grave, having erecting a massive new tombstone engraved with the single word: Richthofen.

During the Cold War, the Invalidenfriedhof was on the boundary of the Soviet zone in Berlin, and the tombstone, sitting just beside a stretch of the Berlin Wall, became damaged by bullets fired at attempted escapees from East Germany. In 1975, Richthofen's remains were moved to the Richthofen family grave plot at the Südfriedhof in Wiesbaden.

Manfred von Richthofen's cortege on its return to Berlin flanked by holders of the Pour le Mérite

Manfred von Richthofen's coffin being carried into the Gnade Kirche, Berlin by holders of the Pour le Mérite.

CHAPTER TWO

Manfred von Richthofen's body lying in state in Gnade Kirche, Berlin after being disinterred. His 'Ordenkissen' showing all his medals and awards, can be seen at the foot of the coffin.

Manfred von Richthofen's grave where he was interred at the 'Invalidenfriedhof' (Invalids Cemetery where many German senior officers are buried) in Berlin after his state funeral

Manfred von Richthofen's slightly overgrown tomb in the 'Invalidenfriedhof' after his remains were removed and re-interred in the family plot in Mainz.

Manfred von Richthofen's room showing his wall full of trophies.

CHAPTER TWO

Above: Close-up of the trophy wall in Richthofen's study.

Right: Close-up of a section of Richthofen's trophy wall.

Post Mortem of Richthofen

The details of the post-mortem examinations of von Richthofen's body are more than a little confusing.

It is accepted that Manfred von Richthofen was flying an all-red Fokker Dr.I Triplane when he crashed in the Somme Valley near Corbie on the 21 April 1918. His body was recovered from the wreckage and taken to a hangar belonging to No. 3 Squadron, Australian Flying Corps at Poulainville, where an examination of the body was held. The body was washed by an orderly and the first superficial post-mortem examination was made by a panel of doctors, consisting of Colonel T. Sinclair, consulting surgeon to the Fourth Army, Captain G. C. Graham, RAMC and Lieutenant G. E. Downs, RAMC, attached to the Air Force. Also present was Colonel J. A. Dixon, consulting physician to the British Fourth Army.

Colonel Sinclair's report is as follows:

> Copy extracts from A.H.File No. 21/13/506
>
> In the Field 22nd April 1918.
>
> We have made a surface examination of Captain Baron von Richthofen and find that there are only the entrance and exit wounds of one rifle bullet on the trunk. The entrance wound is on the right side about the level of the ninth-rib, which is fractured, just in front of the posterior axillary line. The bullet appears to have passed obliquely backwards through the chest striking the spinal column, from which it glanced in a forward direction and issued on the left side of the chest, at a level about two inches higher than its entrance on the right and about in the anterior axillary line.
>
> There was also a compound fracture of the lower jaw on the left side, apparently not caused by a missile – and also some minor bruises of the head and face.

POST MORTEM OF RICHTHOFEN

The body was not opened – these facts were ascertained by probing from the surface wounds.

(Sngd) Thomas Sinclair
Colonel AMS
Consulting surgeon IV Army
BEF

It is assumed that von Richthofen was sitting straight in his cockpit and the aeroplane was in level flight, that being the case, the bullet must have struck him from the right side, fired from an angle that was slightly in front of the body and fired from below.

Captain Graham and Lieutenant Downs submitted a separate report on von Richthofen's death:

Copy extract from A.H.File No. 21/13/506.

We examined the body of Captain Baron von Richthofen on the evening of the 21st instant. We found that he had one entrance and one exit wound caused by the same bullet.

The entrance wound was situated on the right side of the chest in the posterior fold (sic) of the armpit; the exit wound was situated at a slightly higher level near the front of the chest, the point of exit being about half inch below the right (sic) nipple and about three-quarter of an inch external to it. From the nature of the exit wound we think that the bullet passed straight through the chest from right to left, and also slightly forward. Had the bullet been deflected from the spine the exit wound would have been much larger.

The gun firing this bullet must have been situated in the same plane as the long axis of the German machine and fired from the right and slightly behind the right of Captain von Richthofen.

We are agreed that the situation of the entrance and exit wounds are such that they could not have been caused by fire from the ground.

Sngd. G. C. Graham
Captain RAMC
MO i/c 22nd Wing RAF

Sngd. G. E. Downs
Lieut. RAMC
In the Field
22/4/18

Graham and Downs referred to the exit wound being on the right side; if the exit wound was on the right side, it is unlikely that such a wound would have been fatal and it is generally accepted that Graham and Downs had made a mistake.

However, there still remains the last paragraph of their report attributing the fatal bullet to a shot from the air, not the ground. If, as they considered, the bullet had not been deflected by the vertebral column, then the track of the bullet must have been laterally from below and behind the midline. However, the only way that their statement that: 'The gun firing this bullet must have been situated in the same plane as the long axis of the German machine' could be correct if von Richthofen had been twisting his trunk almost 90 degrees to the right and looking sideways or backwards when he was struck.

A Medical Board consisting of Colonel Barber, Major C. L Chapman, Australian Medical Corps, Major D. Blake and Captain E. G. Knox of No 3 Squadron, AFC, examined the body a second time, but there is no record of any report made by this Medical Board. However, in 1935, Colonel Barber wrote a letter to a Mr Bean, who was in the process of writing an article about the death of Richthofen. The underlining is in the original letter:

> Oct 23 1935
>
> My dear Bean,
>
> With reference to your letter of October 14th asking for information.
>
> I was inspecting this Air Force Unit and found the medical orderly washing Richthofen's body so I made an examination. There were only two bullet wounds, one of entry, one of exit of a bullet that had evidently passed through the chest and the heart. There was no wound of the head but there was considerable bruising over the right jaw which may have been fractured. The orderly told me that the consulting surgeon of the Army had made a post-mortem in the morning and I asked how he did it as there was no evidence. The orderly told me that the cons. surgeon used a bit of fencing wire which he had pushed along the track of the wound through over the heart. I used the same bit of wire for the same purpose so you see the medical examination was not a thorough one and not a post-mortem exam in the ordinary

sense of the term. The bullet hole in the side of the plane coincided with the wound through the chest and I am sure he was shot from below while banking.

I sent a full report to General Birdwood at Australian Corps and I have often wondered what became of it.

With kind regards,
Yrs sincerely
George W. Barber

Colonel Barber enclosed a diagram of the bullet wounds on the body with his letter. In this he clearly showed the entrance wound in the left posterior axillary line at about the level of the ninth rib, and drew a cross over the right chest, internal to the nipple on the AP view.

Barber's letter clarifies the probe used by Sinclair, which was not a surgical one; a surgical probe is a rigid piece of metal with a smooth rounded bulbous tip that is designed to avoid making false passages in the tissues. A 'piece of fence wire' is flexible and has a cut end; this would certainly not have been rounded and would have been prone to catch in the tissues, particularly the light air-filled tissues of the lung. Barber's letter, therefore, casts doubt on the accuracy of Sinclair's report. It would have been possible to have used such a probe to examine the exit wound and determine that the bullet track involved the heart, but it would have been quite impossible to determine the track of the bullet to the vertebral column by using such a probe from the entrance wound.

In 1969, O'Dwyer carefully addressed other difficulties in Sinclair's report that the bullet was deflected by the vertebral column. O'Dwyer sought medical opinions on the extreme difficulty in probing lung tissue. The lungs would collapse as soon as air entered the pleural cavity (the space between the lungs and the chest wall), and it would be impossible for a probe to detect any perforation of the lungs made by a bullet.

The conclusion is that the fatal bullet must have passed directly through the chest from its entry wound at the posterior axillary line (the back of the armpit) at the level of the ninth rib (that is at about 5 inches below the lower level of the outstretched arm). As there is no real evidence that the bullet hit the vertebrae, the most probable trajectory of the bullet would have to be along a line joining the entrance and exit wounds. Such a line indicates that the bullet was fired from the side, behind and below the pilot's body, notwithstanding his position in the cockpit.

As the exit wound was about three-quarters of an inch external to the left nipple this means that the bullet would have passed through the heart and would have been rapidly fatal. Von Richthofen would have lost consciousness within twenty to thirty seconds, and certainly could not have continued to fly his aeroplane and fire on Lieutenant May for over a minute.

It is possible to correlate the medical evidence with that of the eyewitnesses of the last flight. Fortunately, as the events took place at low altitude, directly over the Australian lines, many eyewitnesses witnessed the chase and crash.

There is no doubt that von Richthofen followed a Sopwith Camel, flown by a relatively novice Canadian pilot, Lieutenant Wilfred May, down from a dogfight that occurred when two British photographic reconnaissance R.E. 8 aircraft were attacked by von Richthofen's Jasta, west of Hamel. Lieutenants Carisella, and Ryan, the observer and gunner aboard the second R.E. 8, describe the attack in detail. The presence of the German triplanes was seen by a formation of eight Sopwith Camels, led by Captain A. Roy Brown, DSC, a Canadian flying with the newly formed Royal Air Force.

Lieutenant May, who had been told by Brown that he should observe any action, but should run for home if attacked, was seen by von Richthofen and pursued. According to his instructions, May dived away and flew low over the Australian lines, flying down the valley of the Somme, closely pursued by Richthofen. Captain Brown saw the chase and dived from behind on von Richthofen's triplane at about 11 a.m.

The following is Captain Roy Brown's combat report, written after his return to Bertangles airfield:

> *At 10:35 A.M. I observed two Albatross burst into flames and crash. Dived on large formation of fifteen to twenty Albatross scouts D. V.s and Fokker triplanes, two of which got on my tail and I came out. Went back again and dived on pure red triplane which was firing on Lt. May. I got a long burst into him and he went down vertical and was observed to crash by Lieutenant Mellersh and Lieutenant May. I fired on two more but did not get them.*

In a five-part article entitled 'My Fight with Richthofen', which was published in the late 1920s and attributed to Brown, Brown was quoted as having said:

POST MORTEM OF RICHTHOFEN

'I was in a perfect position above and behind. ... neither plane, (Richthofen or May) was aware of me ... I had dived until the red snout of my Camel pointed fair at his tail. My thumbs pressed the triggers. Bullets ripped into his elevator and tail planes. The flaming tracers showed me where they hit. A little short! Gently I pulled back on the stick. The nose of the Camel rose ever so slightly. Easy now, easy. The stream of bullets tore along the body of the all-red tripe [sic]. Its occupant turned and looked back. I had a flash of his eyes behind the goggles. Then he crumpled – sagged in the cockpit ... Richthofen was dead. The triplane staggered, wobbled, stalled, flung over on its nose and went down. The reserve trenches of the Australian infantry was *(sic)* not more than 200 feet below.'

It was a quick descent. Indeed there is only one witness who suggests that Captain Brown shot down the red Fokker triplane, and even this is an indirect statement. Second Lieutenant Mellor, RFC was quoted in the *Melbourne Herald* newspaper of 26 February 1930:

'Captain Brown seeing May's predicament, followed the red Fokker and closing up to a range of about 100 yards, fired a long burst from both guns. I could see his tracer hitting the cockpit of the Fokker. The German machine zoomed, banked steeply and obviously crippled glided down to land between the Allied and German lines. He landed under control so the machine was not damaged.... The Australian Lewis gunners certainly hit the machine but their bullets hit about two feet behind the cockpit.'

Lieutenant Mellersh, who was flying with Brown, was a witness to the crash of the triplane but he did not see Brown engage the Fokker. His account, printed in *Tatler* describes Mellersh as having engine problems and '...I was forced to spindive to the ground and return to our lines at about 50 feet. Whilst so returning a bright red triplane crashed quite close to me and in looking up I saw Captain Brown's machine.'

Despite Brown's statement that the triplane crashed after he had fired on it, von Richthofen did continue to follow May down the Somme valley at a low altitude. He appeared to be completely absorbed in his chase and, as he came within range, he came under fire from Australian anti-aircraft machine guns. In particular there was a Vickers heavy machine gun, under the command of Sergeant Cedric Popkin, which was situated about 1,000 yards west of the village of Vaux on the northern bank of the Somme River, and the 53rd and 54th Batteries of Lewis guns, on anti-aircraft pole mountings, on the eastern slope of a shallow hill about 1,000 yards east of Bonnay.

As he came to the hill, Lieutenant May, hugging the ground contours, rose to clear the rise and flew on in a straight line after passing it. The red triplane, still following May, also rose to clear the hill, but then came under machine-gun fire from the 53rd and 54th Batteries. It then performed an Immelmann turn to return back to the German lines. This aspect of the fight was observed by Gunner George Ridgeway, from Lang Lang in Victoria, who was on top of the Heilly brick stack near the Bray-Corbie road and who had an excellent view. The full text is as follows:

> He states that he was about 200 feet from the ground. The first plane passed to the right and rapidly began to climb. As soon as it was out of danger the machine gunners opened out on the German. Von Richthofen, he claims, came within 200 feet of the ground and to save himself he swerved to the left and immediately banked at an angle of 75 degrees. He was sitting upright in the cabin and could be seen plainly at the controls. All this occurred within 100 yards of the Heilly chimneystack.
>
> The first plane having reached a safe altitude, the German plane provided an excellent target for the machine guns who were in a circle around him at Vaux-sur-Somme, Bonney (sic) and Corbee (sic) and thousands of rounds were fired at him, to use Gunner Ridgway's words, 'A rain of death bespattered him.'
>
> The plane seeking frantically to escape only rose about 500 feet when it turned over to its left, and crashed to the ground.
>
> Gunner Ridgway, who still retains the number plate of the machine was one of the first at the scene. On the number plate are the words: 'Militar Fluzzeug (sic) Fokker DR. 1525/17'. He is emphatic that the Baron was alive when he banked after the other planes had gone. The nearest plane to him was at least half a mile away. He states that there was plenty of evidence to show that Captain Brown did not get

POST MORTEM OF RICHTHOFEN

him and hopes that the official War History will be amended even at this late date.

A. W. Madge
Lang Lang correspondent.

However, although an indirect quotation, Ridgway's reported statement is confirmed by Lieutenant G. M. Travers MC. Travers was observing near 11th Brigade HQ when he heard planes approaching from the direction of 26 central, and heard a Vickers gun firing from the ground. He wrote:

> April 1918.
>
> The first plane that came into view was one of our own, and less than 20 paces behind him was an enemy plane painted red. The red plane was overhauling our plane fast and both were flying so low that they almost crashed into trees at the top of the hill. Almost directly over the spot where I was lying the enemy plane swerved to the right so suddenly that it seemed almost to turn over. Our plane went straight on, from that moment the enemy plane was quite out of control and did a wild circle and dashed towards J.19.b.34 where it crashed. I went over with other officers and had a look at the plane and also the driver, who was dead, a machine-gun bullet had passed from the left side of his face and near bottom of jaw and came out just behind the right eye (16)...The Vickers gun mentioned was the only gun firing at the time the driver first lost control of his machine. I made enquiries and found the gun was handled by No. 424 Sergt. Cedric Basset Popkin, 24 Australian Machine Gun Company.
>
> G. M. Travers Lieut
Company 52nd Bat AEF

Further confirmation that Ridgway's story is correct also came from Lieutenant J. A. Wiltshire, MC who wrote:

> Dear Sir,
>
> In reference to Richthofen's death. Standing on a 'Farm Track' close to the Mericourt, Corbie road about two kilos almost due south of Heilly.

THE RED BARON

> Looking east I saw a fight in progress in the air. Three planes, two British and one German dived out of the fight. The German on both their tails, one British plane dived out towards the Somme, the other with the German on his tail, continued toward the ground out of my sight. Within minutes, from the east, they appeared over the rise and flying about 40 feet from the ground. Passed almost overhead.
>
> The British plane was flying up and down the German flying to imitate and giving quick bursts with his gun. The German pilot seemed to crouch forward as he gave each burst. The British plane had apparently no tail gun, as he did not reply.
>
> The British plane steeplechased a group of trees, and swooped down over the Ancre and continued his course between Bonnay and Heilly to the rear lifting over the trees. The German plane gave up the chase and banking to his left straightened his plane toward his line and commenced to climb. He now came under machinegun fire from the ground. His plane would be just about overhead of the artillery. The plane seemed to steady and then headed slowly for the ground. Landing on the Somme side of the high ground.

Sergeant Popkin's Vickers gun position was situated at the foot of the hill at Bonnay, one kilometre to the south-east of the Lewis gun battery manned by Gunners Buie and Evans, and just to the south of the German triplane's flight path. Popkin was ideally situated to fire on von Richthofen when he turned to the right, away from the fire of the Lewis gun battery on the hill.

Popkin wrote on the 16 October 1935:

> The planes would be travelling in a North East direction straight towards my gun position. I opened fire immediately the British plane left my gun sights and followed the fritz around. He would be perhaps 100 to 120 yards in front of me when I opened fire and about 200 to 400 feet in the air. He would be below the top of the ridge, which is about 500 to 600 feet high. I opened fire the second time at the peak of his turn marked X. I don't think that I was firing so long the second time as the

POST MORTEM OF RICHTHOFEN

first. I would be firing at him the second time while he was travelling the line between the two crosses.

I would be firing about half to three-quarters a minute each time.

I reached the plane just when they were about to place a guard on it.

A chap named Marshall my No. 3 on the gun at the time who was afterwards killed, got a bullet off Richthofen's body which had just penetrated his clothes and half sticking in his skin right on his belt line.

Yours faithfully
C B Popkin

From Popkin's letter it is apparent that Popkin missed when he first opened fire. The German triplane was heading towards him when this happened. He then fired for the second time and was firing as the pilot of the triplane was going away from him whilst banking. This is consistent with Popkin firing a bullet that entered von Richthofen's body at the ninth rib in the posterior axillary line. The angle of Popkin's fire was in accordance with the trajectory of the bullet that killed von Richthofen, that is to say it was in a line from behind the midline of the pilot's trunk and from below,

Further confirmation of Popkin's letter is available from a letter from Popkin's commanding officer, Captain F. R. Watts, in the Bean Papers:

> 19 11 29
>
> Sergeant Popkin allowed the British plane to pass and then fired at Richthofen who made a right swing and then came back to the gun and this time at a lower height when Popkin fired about 200 rounds at him and Richthofen swung round to the right and just managed to clear the ridge and crashed. I can assure you that there was no-one else had a chance to bring him down because there was no other guns close enough except mine.
>
> GUNNER BUIE'S CLAIM
>
> We were free to fire at any time without command, but as the planes neared us barely 50 feet off the brow of the ridge I was

prevented from firing immediately as the two machines were almost in line, with Lt. May's plane blocking my line of fire.

Major Beavis and Lieutenant Doyle were on my right and left respectively, near Evan's gun position, about 30 yards away. Lieutenant Ellis, on slightly lower ground at my centre, observed the oncoming planes from the flank and shouted, 'Fire on that plane, Buie!' But I still could not, owing to Lieutenant May's position.

I was swivelling my gun to follow the red machine, and Snowy Evans, manning the other gun on the opposite flank, got first clearance. He opened up at a range of slightly more than 300 yards. The triplane flew steadily on, still firing short bursts at the Camel it was now barely 20 yards behind and 10 feet above May. Very close indeed. I was at the ready with my finger on the trigger, waiting the clearance. It came.

I can still remember seeing Richthofen clearly. His helmet covered most of his head and face and he was hunched in the cockpit aiming over his guns at the lead plane. It seemed that with every burst he leaned forward in the cockpit as though concentrating very intently on his fire. Certainly he was not aware of his dangerous position or of the close range of our guns. His position was much as a strafing attack would appear, and had he not been so intent upon shooting down Lieutenant May, he could easily have manoeuvred his machine and fired upon us, had he been so inclined. Richthofen and his men frequently strafed our trenches to the east.

At 200 yards, with my peep sight directly on Richthofen's body I began firing with steady bursts. His plane was bearing frontal and just a little to the right of me and after 20 rounds I knew that the bullets were striking the right side and front of the machine, for I clearly saw fragments flying.

Still Richthofen came on firing at Lieutenant May with both guns blazing. Then just before my last shots finished at a range of 40 yards Richthofen's guns stopped abruptly. The thought flashed through my mind – I've hit him! – and immediately I noticed a sharp change in engine sound as the red triplane passed over our gun position at less than 50 feet and still a little to my right. It slackened speed considerably and the propeller slowed down although the machine still appeared to be under control. Then it veered a bit to the right and then back to the left and lost height gradually coming down near an abandoned brick kiln 400 yards away on the Bray-Corbie road.

I looked to my gun. It was empty. I had fired a full pannier....

Buie also commented on the bullet wounds sustained by Richthofen:

A guard was placed over the body and after a while it was brought to our position. Major Beavis claimed the body for the 53rd and it was placed on a nearby stretcher. There I saw it. In the crash Richthofen's face was thrown against the gun butts and suffered minor injuries. Blood had come from his mouth which indicated at first glance that a fatal bullet had pierced a lung.

According to the popular version, death came from a single bullet which had entered his back and passed forward through the chest.

This was not true.

Richthofen was struck in the left breast, abdomen and right knee. I examined these wounds as his body lay on the stretcher. His fur-lined boots were missing, as were his helmet and goggles and other personal effects, these having been taken before his body arrived at the battery. He was wearing silk pyjamas under his flying clothes.

The wounds were all frontal. Their entrances were small and clean and the exit points were slightly larger and irregular in the back. Later, Colonel Barber of the Australian Corps and Colonel Sinclair of the Fourth Army, both medical officers, made separate examinations of the body and their reports agreed that the chest wound was definitely caused by ground fire.

All that we can be sure of is that the entry and exit wounds on von Richthofen's body meant that the bullet passed through the heart, or great vessels, and he could not have remained conscious for more than about thirty seconds after being hit. The fatal bullet had therefore to have been fired at von Richthofen at the end of the pursuit and this is likely to have been at the time when the triplane was observed to turn away from the hill where the Lewis gun batteries were situated.

SUMMARY

The official post-mortem examination report is, in all probability, flawed and it is most likely that the bullet track was along a line joining the entrance and exit wounds. In other words, the bullet came from behind, below and lateral to von Richthofen. There is little doubt that the bullet penetrated his heart and was fatal. Neither Captain Brown nor Gunner Buie could have inflicted such a wound.

The only known gunner that could have done so was Sergeant Popkin when he opened fire for the second time when Richthofen was turning away from him. Richthofen then lost control of his aeroplane and crashed, he was dead when his aeroplane hit the ground.

From the evidence of the post-mortem examination and from eyewitnesses it was therefore most probably Sergeant Popkin who fired the fatal shot, although a lucky shot from an unknown soldier firing his rifle cannot be excluded.

Appendix I

List of Manfred von Richthofen's victories in the First World War

Victim	Date	Richthofen's Unit	Richthofen's Aircraft	Victim's Squadron
1. Lieutenant Lionel Morris (KIA) Lieutenant Tom Rees (Obs) (KIA)	17/09/1916	Jasta 2	Albatros D.II	11 Squadron
2. Sergeant H. Bellerby (KIA)	23/09/1916	Jasta 2	Albatros D.II	27 Squadron
3. Lieutenant E. Conway Lansdale (KIA) Squadron Sergeant A. Clarkson (Obs) (KIA)	30/09/1916	Jasta 2	Albatros D.II	11 Squadron
4. 2nd Lieutenant W. Fenwick (KIA)	07/10/1916	Jasta 2	Albatros D.II	21 Squadron
5. Sergeant S Cockerill (WIA)	16/10/1916	Jasta 2	Albatros D.II	24 Squadron
6. Lieutenant C.R. Tisdale (PoW)	17/10/1916	Jasta 2	Albatros D.II	21 Squadron
7. Sergeant C. Baldwin (KIA) Lieutenant G. Betham Andrew (Obs) (KIA)	03/11/1916	Jasta 2	Albatros D.II	18 Squadron
8. 2nd Lieutenant I. Gilmour Cameron (KIA)	09/11/1916	Jasta 2	Albatros D.II	12 Squadron
9. Lieutenant T. H. Clark (PoW) 2nd Lieutenant James Lees (Obs)(PoW)	20/11/1916	Jasta 2	Albatros D.II	15 Squadron
10. 2nd Lieutenant S. Hall (KIA) 2nd Lieutenant G. Doughty (Obs) (KIA)	20/11/1916	Jasta 2	Albatros D.II	18 Squadron
11. Major Lanoe Hawker (KIA)	23/11/1916	Jasta 2	Albatros D.II	24 Squadron
12. Lieutenant B. Philip Hunt (PoW)	11/12/1916	Jasta 2	Albatros D.II	32 Squadron
13. Captain A.G. Knight (KIA)	20/12/1916	Jasta 2	Albatros D.II	29 Squadron

THE RED BARON

Victim	Date	Richthofen's Unit	Richthofen's Aircraft	Victim's Squadron
14. Lieutenant L.G. D'Arcy (KIA) Sub Lieutenant R. Whiteside RNVR (Obs) (KIA)	20/12/1916	Jasta 2	Albatros D.II	18 Squadron
15. Sergeant J. McCudden (WIA)	27/12/1916	Jasta 2	Albatros D.II	11 Squadron
16. Flight Lieutenant A.S. Todd (Can) (KIA)	4/01/1917	Jasta 2	Albatros D.II	8 RNAS
17. 2nd Lieutenant John Hay (Aus)	23/01/1917	Jasta 11	Albatros D.II	40 Squadron
18. Captain Oscar Greig (PoW) Lieutenant J. McClennan (Obs) (PoW)	27/01/1917	Jasta 11	Albatros D.II	25 Squadron
19. Lieutenant Percival Murray (KIA) Lieutenant D.J. McRae (Can) (Obs) (KIA)	01/02/1917	Jasta 11	Halberstadt D.II	16 Squadron
20. Lieutenant Cyril Bennett (PoW) 2nd Lieutenant H.A. Croft (Obs) (KIA)	14/02/1917	Jasta 11	Halberstadt D.II	2 Squadron
21. Captain H.E. Hartney (WIA) 2nd Lieutenant G.W.B. Hampton (Obs)	14/02/1917	Jasta 11	Halberstadt D.II	20 Squadron
22. Lieutenant J.B.E. Crosbee Sergeant J.E. Prance (Obs) (WIA)	04/03/1917	Jasta 11	Halberstadt D.II	2 Squadron
23. 2nd Lieutenant H.J. Green (KIA) 2nd Lieutenant A.W. Reid (Obs) (KIA)	04/03/1917	Jasta 11	Halberstadt D.II	43 Squadron
24. 2nd Lieutenant G.M. Libby (KIA) Lieutenant G.J.O. Brichta (Can) (Obs) (KIA)	06/03/1917	Jasta 11	Halberstadt D.II	16 Squadron
25. Lieutenant A. J. Pearson (KIA)	09/03/1917	Jasta 11	Halberstadt D.II	29 Squadron
26. 2nd Lieutenant James Smith (KIA) 2nd Lieutenant Edward Byrne (Obs) (KIA)	11/03/1917	Jasta 11	Halberstadt D.II	2 Squadron
27. Lieutenant A.E. Boultbee (KIA) 2nd Airman Frederick King (Obs) (KIA)	17/03/1917	Jasta 11	Halberstadt D.II	25 Squadron
28. 2nd Lieutenant G.M. Watt (KIA) Sergeant E.A. Howlett (Obs) (KIA)	17/03/1917	Jasta 11	Halberstadt D.II	16 Squadron

LIST OF MANFRED VON RICHTHOFEN'S VICTORIES

Victim	Date	Richthofen's Unit	Richthofen's Aircraft	Victim's Squadron
29. Flight Sergeant S. H. Quicke (KIA) 2nd Lieutenant W.J. Lidsey (Obs) (KIA)	21/03/1917	Jasta 11	Halberstadt D.II	16 Squadron
30. Lieutenant R.P. Baker (Can) (PoW)	24/03/1917	Jasta 11	Halberstadt D.II	19 Squadron
31. Lieutenant C. G. Gilbert (PoW)	25/03/1917	Jasta 11	Halberstadt D.II	29 Squadron
32. Lieutenant P.J.G. Powell (KIA) 1st Airman Percy Bonner (Obs) (KIA)	02/04/1917	Jasta 11	Albatros D.III	13 Squadron
33. 2nd Lieutenant A.P. Warren (PoW) Sergeant Reuel Dunn (Obs) (KIA)	02/04/1917	Jasta 11	Albatros D.III	43 Squadron
34. 2nd Lieutenant D.P. McDonald (PoW) 2nd Lieutenant J.I.M. O'Beirne (Obs) (KIA)	03/04/1917	Jasta 11	Albatros D.III	25 Squadron
35. 2nd Lieutenant A.N.Leckler (WIA/PoW) 2nd Lieutenant H.D.K. George (Obs) (KIA)	05/04/1917	Jasta 11	Albatros D.III	48 Squadron
36. Lieutenant A.T. Adams (PoW) Lieutenant D. J. Stewart (Obs) (PoW)	05/04/1917	Jasta 11	Albatros D.III	48 Squadron
37. 2nd Lieutenant G.O. Smart (KIA)	07/04/1917	Jasta 11	Albatros D.III	60 Squadron
38. Lieutenant John Heagerty (PoW) Lieutenant L. Cantle (Obs) (KIA)	08/04/1917	Jasta 11	Albatros D.III	3 Squadron
39. 2nd Lieutenant K.I. MacKenzie (KIA) 2nd Lieutenant Guy Everingham (Obs) (KIA)	08/04/1917	Jasta 11	Albatros D.III	16 Squadron
40. Lieutenant E.C.E Derwin (WIA) Gunner H. Pierson (Obs) (WIA).	11/04/1917	Jasta 11	Albatros D.III	3 Squadron
41. Captain J.M. Stuart (KIA) Lieutenant M.H. Wood (Obs) (KIA)	13/04/1917	Jasta 11	Albatros D.III	59 Squadron
42. Sergeant J.A. Cunniffe (WIA) 2nd Airman W.J. Batten (Obs) (WIA)	13/04/1917	Jasta 11	Albatros D.III	11 Squadron

Victim	Date	Richthofen's Unit	Richthofen's Aircraft	Victim's Squadron
43. 2nd Lieutenant A. H. Bates (KIA) Sergeant W. A. Barnes (Obs) (KIA)	13/04/1917	Jasta 11	Albatros D.III	25 Squadron
44. Lieutenant W. O. Russell (PoW)	14/04/1017	Jasta 11	Albatros D.III	60 Squadron
45. 2nd Lieutenant Alphonso Pascoe (WIA) 2nd Lieutenant F.S. Andrews (Obs) (KIA)	16/04/1917	Jasta 11	Albatros D.III	13 Squadron
46. Lieutenant W. Fletcher (WIA) Lieutenant W.F. Franklin (Obs) (WIA)	22/04/1017	Jasta 11	Albatros D.III	11 Squadron
47. 2nd Lieutenant Eric Welch (KIA) Sergeant A. G. Tollervey (Obs) (KIA)	23/04/1917	Jasta 11	Albatros D.III	16 Squadron
48. Lieutenant R. W. Follit (KIA) 2nd Lieutenant F.J. Kirkham (Obs) (PoW)	28/04/1917	Jasta 11	Albatros D.III	13 Squadron
49. Lieutenant Richard Applin (KIA)	29/04/1917	Jasta 11	Albatros D.III	19 Squadron
50. Sergeant George Stead (KIA) Corporal Alfred Beebee (Obs) (KIA)	29/04/1917	Jasta 11	Albatros D.III	18 Squadron
51. Lieutenant D. E. Davies (KIA) Lieutenant G.H. Rathbone (Obs) (KIA)	29/04/1917	Jasta 11	Albatros D.III	12 Squadron
52. Flight Sub.Lt. A.E. Cuzner (Can) (KIA)	29/04/1917	Jasta 11	Albatros D.III	8 RNAS
53. Lieutenant R.W.E. Ellis (KIA)	18/06/1917	JG 1	Albatros D.V	9 Squadron
54. Lieutenant F. W. Farquhar	23/06/1917	JG 1	Albatros D.V	23 Squadron
55. Captain N.G. McNaughton (KIA) Lieutenant A. H. Mearns (Obs) (KIA)	24/06/1917	JG 1	Albatros D.V	57 Squadron
56. Lieutenant L.S. Bowman (KIA) 2nd Lieutenant J.E. Power-Clutterbuck (Obs) (KIA)	25/06/1917	JG 1	Albatros D.V	53 Squadron
57. Sergeant H.A. Whatley (KIA) 2nd Lieutenant F.G. B. Pascoe Obs) (KIA)	02/07/1917	JG 1	Albatros D.V	53 Squadron

LIST OF MANFRED VON RICHTHOFEN'S VICTORIES

Victim	Date	Richthofen's Unit	Richthofen's Aircraft	Victim's Squadron
58. 2nd Lieutenant W.H.T. Williams (WIA)	16/08/1917	JG 1	Albatros D.V	29 Squadron
59. 2nd Lieutenant C. P. Williams (KIA)	26/08/1917	JG 1	Albatros D.V	19 Squadron
60. Lieutenant J.B.C. Madge (WIA/PoW) 2nd Lieutenant Walter Kember (Obs) (KIA)	01/09/1917	JG 1	Albatros D.V	6 Squadron
61. Lieutenant A. F. Bird (PoW)	03/11/1917	JG 1	Fokker F.1	46 Squadron
62. Lieutenant J.A.V. Boddy (WIA)	23/11/1917	JG 1	Albatros D.V	64 Squadron
63. Lieutenant D.A.D.I. McGregor (KIA)	30/11/1917	JG 1	Albatros D.V	41 Squadron
64. 2nd Lieutenant L.F.C. Clutterbuck (PoW) 2nd Lieutenant H. J. Sparks (Obs) (PoW)	12/03/1918	JG 1	Fokker Dr.1	62 Squadron
65. 2nd Lieutenant J. Millett	13/03/1918	JG 1	Fokker Dr.1	73 Squadron
66. 2nd Lieutenant W.G. Ivamy (Can) (PoW)	18/03/1918	JG 1	Fokker Dr.1	54 Squadron
67. Lieutenant J.P. McCone (Can) (KIA)	24/03/1918	JG 1	Fokker Dr.1	41 Squadron
68. 2nd Lieutenant Donald Cameron (KIA)	25/03/1918	JG 1	Fokker Dr.1	3 Squadron
69. Lieutenant A. M. Denovan (Can) (KIA)	26/03/1918	JG 1	Fokker Dr.1	1 Squadron
70. 2nd Lieutenant V.J. Reading (KIA) 2nd Lieutenant Matthew Leggat (Obs) (KIA)	27/03/1918	JG 1	Fokker Dr.1	15 Squadron
71. Captain T.S. Sharpe (WIA/PoW)	27/03/1918	JG 1	Fokker Dr.1	73 Squadron
72. Captain R.K. Kirkman (PoW) Captain J.H. Hedley (Obs) (PoW)	27/03/1918	JG 1	Fokker Dr.1	20 Squadron
73. 2nd Lieutenant G.H. Harding (USA) (KIA)	27/03/1918	JG 1	Fokker Dr.1	79 Squadron
74. 2nd Lieutenant J.B. Taylor (KIA) 2nd Lieutenant Eric Betley (Obs) (KIA)	28/03/1918	JG 1	Fokker Dr.1	82 Squadron

Victim	Date	Richthofen's Unit	Richthofen's Aircraft	Victim's Squadron
75. 2nd Lieutenant E.D. Jones (KIA) 2nd Lieutenant R. F. Newton (Obs) (KIA)	02/04/1918	JG 1	Fokker Dr.1	52 Squadron
76. Captain S.P. Smith (MIA)	06/04/1918	JG 1	Fokker Dr.1	46 Squadron
77. 2nd Lieutenant A.V. Gallie	07/04/1918	JG 1	Fokker Dr.1	73 Squadron
78. Lieutenant R.G.H. Adams (WIA/PoW)	07/04/1918	JG 1	Fokker Dr.1	73 Squadron
79. Major R. Raymond Barker (KIA)	20/04/1918	JG 1	Fokker Dr.1	3 Squadron
80. 2nd Lieutenant D.G. Lewis (PoW)	20/04/1918	JG 1	Fokker Dr.1	3 Squadron

KIA – Killed in Action
WIA – Wounded in Action
MIA – Missing in Action
PoW – Prisoner of War
Obs – Observer

Appendix II

Rittmeister Manfred Freiherr von Richthofen

Decorations and awards. Listed as they appear in the images throughout the book.

Prussian Pour le Mérite: 12 January 1917 (in recognition of his sixteenth aerial victory).
Prussian Order of the Red Eagle, 3rd Class with Crown and Swords: 6 April 1918 (in recognition of his seventieth aerial victory).
Prussian House Order of Hohenzollern, Knight's Cross with Swords: 11 November 1916.
Prussian Iron Cross, 1st Class (1914): 23 September 1914
Prussian Iron Cross, 2nd Class (1914): 12 September 1914
Bavarian Military Merit Order, 4th Class with Swords: 29 April 1917.
Duke Carl Eduard Medal with Swords clasp: 9 November 1916
War Merit Cross for heroic act (Lippe)
Brunswick War Merit Cross, 2nd Class
Wound Badge (1918) in Black
Saxon Military Order of St. Henry, Knight's Cross: 16 April 1917.
Württemberg Military Merit Order (Württemberg), Knight's Cross: 13 April 1917
Saxe-Ernestine House Order, Knight 1st Class with Swords (issued by the Duchy of Saxe-Coburg and Gotha): 9 May 1917.
Hesse General Honour Decoration, 'for Bravery'
Lippe War Honour Cross for Heroic Deeds, 2nd class: 13 October 1917.
Schaumburg-Lippe Cross for Faithful Service: 10 October 1917.
Bremen Hanseatic Cross: 25 September 1917.
Lübeck Hanseatic Cross: 22 September 1917.
Hamburg Hanseatic Cross
Austrian Order of the Iron Crown, 3rd Class with War Decoration: 8 August 1917.
Austrian Military Merit Cross, 3rd Class with War Decoration.
Bulgarian Order of Bravery, 4th Class (1st Grade): 12 June 1917

THE RED BARON

Turkish Imtiaz Medal in Silver with Sabres
Turkish LIAKAT Medal in Silver with Sabres
Turkish War Medal ('Iron Crescent' or 'Gallipoli Star'): 4 November 1917
German Army Pilot's Badge
German Army Observer's Badge
Austrian Field Pilot's Badge (Franz Joseph pattern)

Richthofen's awards and medals as on the Ordenkissen:

Down Left side: German Army pilots badge, Iron Cross 1st Class, Lippe War Honour Cross for Heroic Deeds, 2nd Class, Bulgarian Order of Bravery, 4th Class (1st Grade).

Centre: Prussian order of the Red eagle, 3rd Class with Crown with crossed swords. Orden Pour le Mérite.

Down Right side: Austria-Hungarian Field Pilots Badge (Franz Joseph Pattern), Turkish War Medal, Turkish Imtiaz Medal in Silver with Sabres,

Centre row: Iron Cross 2nd Class, Prussian House Order of Hohenzollern, Knight's Cross with Swords, Saxon Military Order of St. Henry, Knight's Cross, Saxe-Ernstine House Order, Knight's 1st Class with Swords, Bavarian Military Merit Order, 4th Class with Swords, Württemberg Military Merit Order, Knight's Cross, Duke Carl Eduard Medal with Swords clasp, Hesse General Honour Decoration for Bravery, Schaumber-Lippe Cross for faithful Service, Brunswick War Merit Cross, 2nd Class, Lübeck Hanseatic Cross, Hamburg Hanseatic Cross, Bremen Hanseatic Cross, Austrian Order of the Iron Crown, 3rd Class with War Decoration, Austrian Military Merit Cross, 3rd Class with War Decoration.

Glossary

A.Fl.Pk,	Army Flieger Park	Army Aviation Replacement Park
AFP	Army Flug Park	Aviation Supply Depot
Boghol	Bombengeschwader	Bombing Unit
Cie	Escadrille	French Balloon Company
Esc	Escadrille	French/Belgian Squadron
FA	Flieger Abteilung	Flying Unit/Section
FA(A)	Flieger Abteilung Artillerie	Flying Unit Artillery
FEA	Flieger Ersatz Abteilung	Pilot Training Unit
FFA	Feldflieger Abteilung	Field Aviation Unit
Fr	Freiherr	Baron
Jasta	Jagdstaffel	Fighting Unit/Squadron
JaSch	Jastaschule	Fighter Pilot School
JG	Jagdgeschwader	Permanent Group of Jastas
JGr	Jagdgruppe	Temporary Group of Jastas
Kaghol	Kampfgeschwader	Combat Squadron
Kasta	Kampfstaffel	Fighting Section
Kek	Kampfeinsitzerkommando	Group of Fighting Planes
Kest	Kampfeinsitzer Staffeln	Home Defence Squadron
KG	Kampfgeschwader	Bombing Squadron
Kofl	Kommandeur der Flieger	CO of Armee Aviation
MFJ	Marine Feld Jasta	Marine Fighting Unit
SFS	Seefrontstaffel	Marine Unit
SSt	Schutzstaffel	Ground Support Unit

Index

Adams, Lieutenant A.T., 144
Adams, Lieutenant R.G.H., 147
Albatros C.II, 7, 18
Albatros C.IX, 22
Albatros D.I, 8, 23
Albatros D.II, 18, 22–5, 142
Albatros D.III, 10, 18–19, 27, 30, 37, 57, 68, 96, 143–5
Albatros D.V, 39, 54–5, 58–9, 63–4, 70–71, 75, 80, 95–6, 98–9, 132, 145–6
Allmenröder, Leutnant Karl, 28, 39, 57
Althaus, Oberstleutnant Ernst Freiherr von, 13, 54
Ancre, 26
Andrew, Lieutenant Betham G., 141
Andrews, 2nd Lieutenant F.S., 144
Applin, Lieutenant Richard, 145
Arnim, General Sixt von, 92–3
Arras, 11
Artillery, 53rd Battery Australian Field, 17
Auer, Leutnant August, 56, 70
Austria, 3
Austro-Hungarian, 2

Bad Homburg, 47–50
Baker, (Can), Lieutenant R.P., 143
Baldwin, Sergeant C., 141
BAO (Brieftauben-Abteilung-Ostende), 8
Bapaume, 8
Barber, Colonel George, 130–1, 138
Barker, Major R. Raymond, 147
Barnes, Sergeant W.A., 144
Bates, 2nd Lieutenant A.H., 144
Batten, 2nd Airman W.J., 144
Bauer, Oberleutnant, 76
BE.2d, 29–30
BE.2c, 45
BE.2e, 28
BE.12, 23
Beavis, Major, 138–9
Beebee, Corporal Alfred, 145
Belgium, 2
Bellerby, Sergeant H., 141
Bender, Leutnant, 56
Bennett, Lieutenant C., 143
Berlin, 47, 123–5
Berlin Wall, 123
Berlin War Academy, 4
Bertangles, 114, 123
Berthold, Oberleutnant Oskar, 76–7
Bertincourt, 18, 23, 65
Bethge, Oberleutnant Hans, 7, 67
Betley, 2nd Lieutenant Eric, 146
Bevar, Leutnant, 11

INDEX

Bird, Lieutenant A.F., 14, 32, 81–2, 146
Birdwood, General, 131
Blake, Major D., 130
Bodenshatz, Oberleutnant Karl, 54, 56, 121
Boddy, Lieutenant J.A.V., 146
Boelcke, Hauptmann Oswald, 9, 12, 18, 21–3, 25–6
Boelcke, Hauptmann Wilhelm, 18
Boelcke, Jagdstaffel, 28
Böhme, Leutnant Erwin, 7–9, 18–19, 25
Boistrancourt, 71
Bonnay, 136
Bonner, 1st Airman Percy, 143
Bosnia, 1–2
Bosnian-Serb, 3
Boultbee, Lieutenant A.E., 143
Bowman, Lieutenant L.S., 145
Brauneck, Leutnant Otto, 38–9, 57
Bray-Corbie, 134, 139
Brichta, (Canada), Lieutenant G.O., 143
Britain, 2
Brown, Captain Roy, 103, 113–14, 132–3
Buie, Gunner, 103, 114, 136–8
Byrne, 2nd Lieutenant Edward, 143

Cantle, Lieutenant L., 144
Cambrai, 18, 25
Cameron, 2nd Lieutenant Donald, 146
Cameron, 2nd Lieutenant I. Gilmour, 141
Cappy, 97–8
Carganico, Hauptmann Victor, 12–13, 15
Carisella, Lieutenant, 132

Champagne, 9, 16
Chapman AMC, Major C.L., 130
Clark, Lieutenant T.H., 142
Clarkson, Squadron Sergeant A., 141
Clutterbuck, 2nd Lieutenant L.F.C., 146
Cockerill, Sergeant S., 141
Cologne, 65–6
Corbie, 102, 128, 134–5
Coutrai, 13–14, 76, 81
Croft, 2nd Lieutenant, 142
Crosbee, Lieutenant J.B.E., 142
Cunniffe, Sergant J.A., 144
Cuzner, (Canada), Flight Sub-Lieutenant A.E., 145

D'Arcy, Lieutenant A.G., 142
Davies, Lieutenant D.E., 145
Denovan, (Canada), Lieutenant A.M., 146
Derwin, Lieutenant E.C.E., 144
Dixon, Colonel J.A., 128
Döberitz, 12
Döring, Oberleutnant von, 54
Dostler, Oberleutnant von, 60–1, 76–7
Douaumont, 16
Douai, 27
Doughty, 2nd Lieutenant G., 142
Downs, RAMC, Lieutenant G.E., 128–9
Doyle, Lieutenant, 138
Dunn, Sergeant Reuel, 143
Dyson, Lieutenant Will, 102

Eastern Front, 7
Einen, General von, 9
Ellis, Lieutenant R.W.E., 145
Epinoy, 10–11, 46

Esser, Leutnant Karl, 39, 44, 57
Evans, Gunner, 103, 136, 138
Everingham, 2nd Lieutenant Guy, 144
Eversbusch, Ernst, 70
Eversbusch, Alfred, 69–70

Falkenhyn, Oberleutnant Fritz, 49–50, 70
Farquar, Lieutenant F.W., 145
Fenwick, 2nd Lieutenant W., 141
Ferdinand, Archduke, 1–2
Festner, Vizefeldwebel, 37, 41, 57
Fisher, 2nd Lieutenant A.J., 141
Flanders, 64, 75, 99
Flashar, Oberleutnant Richard 63–5, 71–2
Fletcher, Lieutenant W., 144
Fokker, Anthony, 90–5
Fokker D.II, 10
Fokker E Type, 16
Fokker Eindecker, 9
Fokker Dr.I Triplane, 28–9, 42, 55, 81, 87, 89–90, 93, 95, 98, 101, 103, 105, 107–108, 110–11, 114, 122, 128, 132–3, 146–7
Fokker D.VII, 15, 95
Fokker E.III, 10, 17
Follit, Lieutenant R.W., 145
Forbeck-Gablenz, 49
Franklin, Lieutenant W.F., 144
Fricourt, 123

Gallie, 2nd Lieutenant A.V., 147
George, 2nd Lieutenant H.D.K., 144
Germany, 2, 20
Gerstenberg, Leutnant Alfred, 15, 46, 64
Ghistelles, 8, 12
Gilbert, Lieutenant C.G., 143
Gille, Unteroffizier, 10
Gontermann, Leutnant Heinrich, 87
Grafe, Leutnant Winand, 23
Graham, RAMC, Captain G.C., 128–9
Grande Kirche, 124–5
Grassman, Leutnant, 56
Green, 2nd Lieutenant H.J., 143
Greig, RFC, Captain Oscar, 142
Grigo, Vizefeldwebel, 11
Gunther, Oberleutnant, 20–2
Gürke, Leutnant Wilhelm, 85

Haehnelt, Oberleutnant Wilhelm, 44
Halberstadt D.II, 142–3
Hall, 2nd Lieutenant S., 142
Hallerstein, Freiherr Hans Haller von, 6
Hamel, 132
Hampton, 2nd Lieutenant G.W.B., 142
Hangard, 16
Harding, (USA), 2nd Lieutenant J.H., 146
Hartmann, Leutnant Otto, 39
Hartney, Captain H.F., 142
Hawker, Major Lanoe, 142
Hay, 2nd Lieutenant John, 142
Heagerty, Lieutenant John, 144
Hedley, Captain J.H., 146
Heilly, 135–6
Heldman, Leutnant, 56
Henin Letard, Alsace, 11
Hinche, Leutnant Hans, 54
Hintsch, Leutnant Hans, 12, 39, 57
Hindenberg, Field marshal von, 47
Hipple, Leutnant Joachim von, 63, 71
Hoeppner, General von, 38, 47–8
Höhene, Leutnant, 21–2

INDEX

Holck, Oberleutnant, 8
Holzapfel, Josef, 13
Howe, Vizefeldwebel, 28
Howlett, Sergeant E.A., 143
Hunt, Lieutenant B. Philip, 142

Immelmann, 21, 27
Invalidenfriedhof, 123, 125–6
Ivamy, (Can) 2nd
    Lieutenant W.G., 146

Jagdstaffel Boelcke, 10
Jagdstaffel 11, 9, 11
Jagdstaffelns 4, 12
Jagdstaffelns 6, 12
Jagdstaffelns 10, 12
Jagdstaffelns 11, 12
Jagdgeschwader (JG), 12–13
Jagdgeschwader 1, 14–15, 19–20
Jasta 2, 8
Jasta 4, 13
Jasta 5, 8, 16–17
Jasta 6, 13
Jasta 10, 10
Jasta 11, 10–11 13, 15
Jasta 12, 11
Jones, 2nd Lieutenant E.D., 146

Kaiser, 47, 76–8
Kaiserin, 48–50
Kasta 8, 6
Kampfeinsitzerkommandos
    (KEK), 16
Kember, 2nd Lieutenant Walter, 145
KG 1 (Kaghol), 6–7
KG 2, 6–7
King, 2nd Airman Frederick, 143
Kintsch, Leutnant Hans, 38
Kirkham, 2nd Lieutenant F.J., 145

Kirkman, Captain R.K., 146
Kirmaier, Oberleutnant Stephan,
    20–2, 25, 27
Knight, Captain A.G., 142
Knox, AFC, Major E.G., 130
Koenig, Leutnant, 20–1
Köln (Cologne), 4
Könitz, Leutnant Freiherr von, 6
Kowel (Kovel), 7, 18
Kranth, Oberleutnant, 76
Krefft, Oberleutnant Henning, 94
Krefft, Leutnant Konstantin, 38–9,
    46–7, 49–51, 57, 62, 70, 87
Kühn, Leutnant Albert, 56

Lagincourt, 22
Lang Lang, Victoria, 134
Lansdale, Lieutenant E.
    Conway, 141
Lechelle, 97
Leckler, 2nd Lieutenant A.N., 144
Lees, 2nd Lieutenant James, 142
Leggat, 2nd Lieutenant Matthew 146
Lehmann, Leutnant Wilhelm,
    63–4, 72
Leib-Kürassier Regiment, 3
Lewis, RFC, 2nd Lieutenant D.G., 147
LFG Factory, 61
LFG Roland D.III, 61
Libby, 2nd Lieutenant G.M., 143
Lichterfelde, 4
Lidsey, 2nd Lieutenant W.J., 143
Lischke, Leutnant Sigfried, 98
Lossberg, Major General Friedrich
    von, 90–1
Löwenhardt, Oberleutnant Erich,
    13, 56, 98
Ludendorff, General Erich, 47, 80
LVG C.II, 16

Madge, A.W., 135
Madge, Lieutenant J.B.C., 145
Mainz, 126
Marckbek, 78, 89–90
Martinsyde G.102, 23
May, Lieutenant Wilfred, 101, 114, 132–3, 138
McCone (Can), Lieutenant J.P., 146
McCudden, Sergeant J., 142
McDonald, 2nd Lieutenant D.P., 143
McGregor, Lieutenant D.A.D.J., 146
McKenzie, 2nd Lieutenant K.I., 144
McLennan, Lieutenant J., 142
McNaughton, Captain N.G., 145
McRay (Canada), Lieutenant D.J., 142
Meams, Lieutenant A.H., 145
Melbourne Herald, 133
Mellersh, Lieutenant, 133
Mellor, RFC, 2nd Lieutenant, 133
Menzke, Corporal, 12
Mericourt, 135
Meyer, Hauptmann Willy, 70
Michaelis, Chancellor Georg, 88–9, 91–3
Millet, 2nd Lieutenant J., 146
Mohnike, Leutnant Eberhard, 44, 83, 84
Mont-Murville, 12
Moorseele, 66
Moritz, 12–14
Morris, RFC, Lieutenant Lionel, 141
Mühlig-Hoffman, Hauptmann Albert, 70
Müller, Leytnant Alfred, 66
Müller, Hauptmann Kurt, 7
Müller, Vizefeldwebel, 23

Müller, Offizierstellverter Max, 20, 40
Murray, Lieutenant Percival, 142

Newton, 2nd Lieutenant R.F., 146
Nieuport 27, 96

O'Beirne, 2nd Lieutenant J.I.M., 143
Ordenkissen, 26, 149
Ostende, 8
Osterroht, Oberleutnant Paul Henning von, 9–11
Osten, Leutnant von der, 40, 44
Otersdorf, Nurse Kate, 60

Parschau, Leutnant, 7
Pasco, 2nd Lieutenant Alphonso, 145
Pascoe, 2nd Lieutenant F.G.B., 144
Pastor, Leutnant, 87
Pearson, Lieutenant A.J., 143
Pechman, Leutnant Paul Freiherr von, 77
Pelzer, Leutnant, 23
Pfalz Dr.I, 69
Pfalz E, 15
Pfalz Factory, 69–70, 81
Pierson, Gunner H., 144
Pluschow, Leutnant Gunther, 39
Popkin, Sergeant Cedric, 103–105, 114, 134, 136–7
Poulainville, 18, 21
Powell, Lieutenant P.J.G., 143
Power-Clutterbuck, 2nd Lieutenant J.E., 145
Prance, Sergeant J.F., 142
Princip, Gavrilo, 1, 2
Prussian, 2

INDEX

Quicke, Flight Sergeant S.H., 143

Rathbone, Lieutenant G.A., 145
Reading, 2nd Lieutenant V.J., 146
Rees, Lieutenant Tom, 141
Regiment, 1st Uhlans Kaiser Alexander III, 4
Regiment, Leib-Kurassier, 3
Regiment Uhlan, 4
Reid, 2nd Lieutenant A.W., 143
Reimann, Leutnant Hans, 17, 23
Reinhard, Oberleutnant Wilhelm, 40, 122–3
Reiss, Leutnant, 98
Rees, Lieutenant Tom, 141
Richthofen, Baroness Kunigunde von, 3, 53
Richthofen, Bolko von, 53
Richthofen's Flying Circus, 54–5, 97, 100
Richthofen Ilse, 4, 53
Richthofen, Lothar von, 4, 11–12, 14, 20, 32, 40, 42–7, 53, 57, 84–5, 123
Richthofen, Major Albrecht von, 20, 45, 53, 84, 123
Richthofen, Wolfram von, 98, 101
Ridgeway, Gunner George, 134
Roland C.II (Walfisch), 16–17
Roucourt, 18, 36–7, 41, 45, 99
Russell, Lieutenant W.O., 144
Russia, 2
Rumney, Leutnant Fritz, 72
Rumpler C.I, 18
Russia, 3
Ryan, Lieutenant, 132

Sailly-le-See, Somme, 120
Sains-le-Marquion, 19

Sandel, Leutnant, 20–1
Sarajevo, 1
Schäfer, Oberleutnant Karl Emil, 41, 56
Schaumberg, Leutnant, 64, 72
Schiffer, Leutnant, 57
Schelegel, Ernst, 69–70
Schloemer, Leutnant, 63
Schramm, Leutnant, 7
Schroeder, Leutnant, 57
Schock, Leutnant, 11
Scholz, Vizefeldwebel, 98
Scholtz, Leutnant, 98
Schweidnitz, 32
Schwerk, Leutnant Victor, 43
Schwerin-Gorries, 51–2, 94–5
SE.5, 85
SE.5a, 15–16
Serbia, 1
Serg, Leutnant Maximilian, 38
Sharpe, Captain T.S., 146
Simon, Leutnant, 57
Sinclair, RAMC, Colonel T., 128–9, 131
Smith, Captain S.P., 146
Smart, 2nd Lieutenant G.O., 144
Smith, 2nd Lieutenant James, 143
Somme, 101, 128, 133
Sopwith Camel F.I, 98, 103, 132
Sopwith Pup, 81, 83–4
Sopwith 1½ Strutters, 19
Sopwith Triplanes, 57
SPAD (Société Pour L'Aviation et ses Dérivés), 55, 96
Sparks, 2nd Lieutenant H.J., 146
Spranger, Hauptmann, 66
Stead, Sergeant George, 145
Steinhauser, Leutnant Werner, 98
Stewart, Lieutenant D.J., 144

Stuart, Captain J.M., 144
Südfriedhof, 20

Tatler, 133
Taylor, 2nd Lieutenant J.B., 146
Thomsen, Oberleutnant, 48
Thüna, Hauptmann Freiherr von, 10
Tisdale, Lieutenant C.R., 141
Todd, (Canada) Flight Lieutenant A.S., 142
Tollervey, Sergeant A.G., 145
Travers, MC, Lieutenant G.M., 135
Tutschek, Oberleutnant Adolf Ritter von, 70

Vaux-sur-Somme, 134
Vauz, 134
Verdun, 12, 16–17
Victoria, 133
Vorhaus, 74
Voss, Leutnant Werner, 14–15, 85–6

Wahlstatt, 3
Walz, Hauptmann, 25
Warren, 2nd Lieutenant A.P., 143
Watt, 2nd Lieutenant G.M., 143
Watts, Captain F.R., 137
Weiss, Leutnant Hans, 98
Welch, 2nd Lieutenant Eric, 145
Western Front, 16
Whatley, Sergeant H.A., 145
Whiteside RNVR, Sub-Lieutenant R., 142
Wicznjace, 8
Wiesbaden, 123
Wilberg, Hauptman Helmuth, 40, 78
Williams, 2nd Lieutenant C.P., 145
Williams, 2nd Lieutenant W.H.T., 145
Wiltshire, MC, Lieutenant J.A., 135
Wolff, Leutnant Kurt, 39, 41, 51–2, 55–7, 86, 94
Wolff, Leutnant Joachim, 98
Wood, Lieutenant M.H., 144
Wortman, Leutnant, 21, 27
Wusthoff, Leutnant Kurt, 40

Zeummer, Oberleutnant Georg, 7–9, 12
Zimmer, Hauptmann Otto, 74

1 Squadron, RFC, 146
2 Squadron, RFC, 30, 142–3
3 Squadron, AFC, 98, 128, 130, 144, 147
6 Squadron, RFC, 145
9 Squadron, RFC, 145
11 Squadron, RFC, 141–2, 144
12 Squadron, RFC, 141, 145
13 Squadron, RFC, 143–5
15 Squadron, RFC, 142, 146
16 Squadron, RFC, 142–5
18 Squadron, RFC, 141–2, 145
19 Squadron, RFC, 143, 145
20 Squadron, RFC, 142, 146
21 Squadron, RFC, 141
24 Squadron RFC, 21–2, 141–2
25 Squadron, RFC, 142–4
27 Squadron, RFC, 141
29 Squadron, RFC, 142–3, 145
32 Squadron, RFC, 142
40 Squadron RFC, 142
41 Squadron, RFC, 146
43 Squadron, RFC, 141, 143

INDEX

46 Squadron, RFC, 146
48 Squadron, RFC, 144
52 Squadron, RFC, 146
53 Squadron, RFC, 145
57 Squadron, RFC, 145
59 Squadron, RFC, 144
60 Squadron, RFC, 144
62 Squadron, RFC, 146
64 Squadron, RFC, 146
73 Squadron, RFC, 146–7
79 Squadron, RFC, 146
82 Squadron, RFC, 146